FIELD GUIDE TO ON-FARM COMPOSTING

Edited by

Mark Dougherty
Former NRAES Staff Engineer

Natural Resource, Agriculture, and Engineering Service (NRAES)
Cooperative Extension • 152 Riley-Robb Hall
Ithaca, New York 14853-5701

NRAES–114
April 1999

ISBN 0-935817-39-5

Library of Congress Cataloging-in-Publication Data

Field guide to on-farm composting / edited by Mark Dougherty.
    p.   cm.   — (NRAES ; 114)
    Includes bibliographical references.
    ISBN 0-935817-39-5 (pbk.)
    1. Compost—Handbooks, manuals, etc.   I. Dougherty, Mark, 1957–
    II. Series : NRAES (Series) ; 114.
    S661.F54   1999
    631.8'75—dc21   98–55088

Natural Resource, Agriculture, and Engineering Service (NRAES)
Cooperative Extension • 152 Riley-Robb Hall
Ithaca, New York 14853-5701
Phone: (607) 255-7654 • *Fax:* (607) 254-8770
E-mail: NRAES@CORNELL.EDU • *Web site:* NRAES.ORG

Reviewers

This publication has been peer-reviewed by the persons listed below. It was judged to be technically accurate and useful for cooperative extension programs and for the intended audience.

- Robert G. Diener
  Professor
  Resource Management Division
  College of Agriculture, Forestry, and Consumer Sciences
  West Virginia University

- Robert E. Graves
  Professor
  Department of Agricultural and Biological Engineering
  The Pennsylvania State University

- Richard Kashmanian
  Senior Economist
  U.S. Environmental Protection Agency

- Scott McCoy
  Composting Program Specialist
  Texas Natural Resource Conservation Commission

- Daniel J. Meyer
  Agricultural Engineering Field Specialist
  Iowa State University Extension

- Joe M. Regenstein
  Professor
  Department of Food Science
  Cornell University

- Tom L. Richard
  Assistant Professor
  Department of Agricultural and Biosystems Engineering
  Iowa State University

- Robert F. Rynk
  Assistant Professor and Extension Engineer
  Department of Biological and Agricultural Engineering
  University of Idaho

- Maarten van de Kamp
  Composting Program Leader
  Massachusetts Department of Food and Agriculture
  University of Massachusetts–Amherst

Contents

List of Figures .... *vii*

List of Tables .... *viii*

List of Photographs .... *ix*

Foreword .... *x*

Introduction 1
  What Happens during Composting? 1
  Advantages of On-Farm Composting 1
  About This Guide 2
  Overview of Composting Methods 2
    Passive or Open-Pile Composting 3
    Turned Windrows and Piles 3
    Aerated Static Piles 5
    In-Vessel Systems 5

Chapter 1: Operations and Equipment 7

This chapter reviews basic operations and equipment needed for on-farm composting, including grinding, shredding, mixing, turning, curing, screening, blending, bagging, and storing. A table showing capacity and power requirements for diverse composting equipment is provided at the end of the chapter.

  Feedstock Preparation 7
    Grinding and Shredding 7
  Mixing and Pile Formation 10
  Active Composting 15
  Compost Curing 15
  Screening 17
  Storing and Packaging 19
    Blending Amendments 20
    Bagging 21

Chapter 2: Raw Materials and Recipe Making 26

This chapter presents a brief description of the most common raw materials used for on-farm composting. A special section, "Advice for First-Time Composters," is also included. Easy-to-read tables and standard formulas are provided to assist in making a compost recipe. At the end of the chapter, a table of commonly used raw materials and their characteristics is presented.

  Raw Materials 26
    Manure as a Composting Material 26
  Advice for First-Time Composters 29
    Balancing Moisture Content and C:N Ratio 30
    The Importance of Porosity 31
    Bulking Materials 31
    The Significance of Pile Heating 32
    Additives 32
    Odors 32
    pH Adjustment 33
    Working with Laboratory Reports 33
  Recipe Making 34
    Balancing Moisture 34
    Balancing Nutrients 37
    Converting Weight Ratios to Volume Ratios 39

Contents

Chapter 3: Process Control and Evaluation 44

This chapter reviews the basic requirements needed to manage active compost. The section on process control emphasizes the necessary biological conditions. The section on process evaluation includes segments on pile sampling, laboratory testing, process monitoring, recordkeeping, and troubleshooting. At the end of the chapter is a handy troubleshooting guide.

Process Control 44
    Managing Biological Activity 44
    Managing Pathogens 47
Process Evaluation 48
    Sampling and Laboratory Testing 48
    Monitoring and Recordkeeping 49
    Troubleshooting 52

Chapter 4: Site Considerations, Environmental Management, and Safety 61

This chapter is divided into three sections: site selection, nuisance control, and safety and accident prevention. The chapter begins by presenting some basic site considerations, including buffer zones and area requirements for windrows. In the second section, management practices for controlling environmental and other nuisances are outlined. At the end of the chapter, safety issues such as equipment safety, accident prevention, operator health, spills, and fires are addressed.

Site Considerations 61
    Buffer Zones 61
    Area Requirements 61
Nuisance Control 62
    Odor Control 62
    Runoff and Leachate Control 68
    Vector Control 69
    Dust Control 70
    Noise Control 70
Safety and Accident Prevention 70
    Operator Health 71
    Spills and Standing Water 72
    Fires 72

Chapter 5: Composting Livestock and Poultry Mortalities 74

This chapter outlines the procedures for composting animal mortalities. Planning, construction, and management practices are explained for three different mortality composting systems: (1) minicomposters, (2) two-bin systems, and (3) composting of catastrophic mortalities. At the end of the chapter, the following environmental and regulatory issues are presented: groundwater and surface water protection, biosecurity, odor, insects, scavengers, and utilization of animal mortality compost.

Compost Process for Animal Mortalities 74
    Ingredients 75
    Moisture 75
    Management 75
Mortality Composting Systems 76
    Minicomposters 76
    Two-Bin System 77
    Composting Catastrophic Mortalities 80

Contents

Chapter 5: Composting Livestock and Poultry Mortalities *(continued)*
Environmental and Regulatory Issues 82
    Groundwater and Surface Water Protection 82
    Biosecurity 83
    Odor, Insects, and Scavengers 83
    Utilizing Mortality Compost 84

Chapter 6: Compost Utilization on the Farm 85

This chapter presents some important characteristics and benefits of farm composts, as well as a brief overview of the most common uses of compost on the farm. At the end of the chapter is a brief section on compost application designed to aid farmers in managing field applications.

Compost Characteristics 85
    Organic Matter Content 85
    Nutrient Content 85
    Stability 86
    Pathogens and Weed Seeds 86
    Particle Size and Texture 86
    pH 86
    Water-Holding Capacity 86
    Moisture Content 87
    Bulk Density 87
    Seed Germination and Plant Growth Response 87
    Soluble Salt Content 87
    Trace Elements 87
    Inerts 88
Farm Use of Compost 88
    As a Source of Nutrients and Soil Amendment for
    Field Crops 88
    For Disease Suppression in Horticultural Production 90
    For Increased Pasture Quality 91
    As a Mulch in Fruit Production 91
Application Rates 92

Appendix A: Case Study–Land Applying Composted Materials and Uncomposted Yard Trimmings on Highly Erodible Land 98

Appendix B: Metric Conversions 105

Photographs 108

References 115

List of Figures

Introduction

Figure 1a   Natural (passive) air movement in a composting pile or windrow 3

Figure 1b   Pull-type windrow turner in operation 4

Figure 1c   Aerated static pile layout 5

Chapter 1: Operations and Equipment

Figure 1-1   Belt-type shear shredder 9

Figure 1-2   Mixing and pile formation with a bucket loader 10

Figure 1-3   Buck wall design for mixing area 11

Figure 1-4   Selected windrow shapes and dimensions 11

Figure 1-5   Suggested windrow spacings 12

Figure 1-6   Dump truck used to form windrows 14

Figure 1-7   Side-delivery, flail-type manure spreader 14

Figure 1-8   Aerobic composting 15

Figure 1-9   Moving stored compost with a bucket loader 20

Figure 1-10   Open-sided storage for finished compost 20

Chapter 3: Process Control and Evaluation

Figure 3-1   Pile and windrow shapes for moisture control 45

Figure 3-2   Beneficial macrofauna observed in composts 47

Figure 3-3   Sample laboratory report 50

Figure 3-4   Instruments for measuring windrow/pile temperatures 51

Figure 3-5   Sample form for monitoring and recording pile information 51

Figure 3-6   Oxygen-analyzing equipment 53

Chapter 4: Site Considerations, Environmental Management, and Safety

Figure 4-1   Grassed filter area for treating compost pad runoff 69

Chapter 5: Composting Livestock and Poultry Mortalities

Figure 5-1   Primary treatment bin in two-bin system 77

Figure 5-2   Maryland freestanding, two-stage composter 79

Figure 5-3   Carcass layering for windrow composting of animal mortality 82

Chapter 6: Compost Utilization on the Farm

Figure 6-1   Field application of compost 94

List of Tables

Chapter 1: Operations and Equipment

Table 1-1   Materials and equipment used for preparing compost feedstock 7

Table 1-2   Recommended conditions for active composting 8

Table 1-3   Approximate volume, in cubic yards, per 100 feet of windrow 12

Table 1-4   Equipment for screening and refining operations 18

Table 1-5   Selected compost equipment: available capacity and horsepower ranges 22

Chapter 2: Raw Materials and Recipe Making

Table 2-1   Type and value of raw ingredients 27

Table 2-2   Production and characteristics of fresh manure (as produced with no bedding or water added) 30

Table 2-3   Preliminary recipe making for two ingredients using only moisture content 35

Table 2-4   Bulk density factors used to convert weight ratios into volume ratios 42

Table 2-5   Typical characteristics of selected raw materials 43

Chapter 3: Process Control and Evaluation

Table 3-1   Troubleshooting guide 55

Chapter 4: Site Considerations, Environmental Management, and Safety

Table 4-1   Commonly recommended separation distances for composting facilities 61

Chapter 5: Composting Livestock and Poultry Mortalities

Table 5-1   Sample compost recipe for composting poultry mortality 79

Table 5-2   Nutrients in built-up (12-flock) litter and dead bird compost 84

Chapter 6: Compost Utilization on the Farm

Table 6-1   Example of compost quality guidelines based on end use 89

Table 6-2   Cubic yards per acre for various depths of application 94

Table 6-3   Application rate, in cubic yards per acre, based on bulk density 96

List of Photographs

Introduction

Photo 1a   Loader lifting and turning 108
Photo 1b   Various pieces of equipment 108
Photo 1c   Small one-pass windrow turner (California)...... 108
Photo 1d   Windrow turner 109
Photo 1e   Aerated static piles 109
Photo 1f   "Ag-bag" composting system 109
Photo 1g   Rotating drum vessel on a dairy (Texas) 109

Chapter 1: Operations and Equipment

Photo 1-1   Windrows on a dairy (Texas) 110
Photo 1-2   Straight windrows on a farm 110
Photo 1-3   Dump truck moving heated material 110
Photo 1-4   Homemade trommel screen (Canada) 110
Photo 1-5   Compost storage shed 111

Chapter 2: Raw Materials and Recipe Making

Photo 2-1   Pile of straw (Idaho).. 111
Photo 2-2   Tare dirt and onion culls 111
Photo 2-3   Potato culls 111
Photo 2-4   Cranberry processing waste 112
Photo 2-5   Spreader with spinners 112
Photo 2-6   Shovelful of compost 112

Chapter 3: Process Control and Evaluation

Photo 3-1   Moisture addition while turning at a dairy
             (Texas)... 112
Photo 3-2   Active composting site in winter 113
Photo 3-3   Maturity tests 113
Photo 3-4   Wet site conditions (advantage of a
             paved site) 113

Chapter 4: Site Considerations, Environmental Management, and Safety

Photo 4-1   Runoff collection ditch 113

Chapter 5: Composting Livestock and Poultry Mortalities

Photo 5-1   Bin composting (Maryland) 114

Foreword

by Scott McCoy, Composting Program Specialist,
Texas Natural Resource Conservation Commission

Composting is as old as life itself. From the time when the first leaf fell and started to decompose, organic matter has been the "glue" that holds fertile soil together. When organic matter is depleted, erosion is more likely. Soil erosion robs American farmers of more than three billion tons of topsoil every year. Runoff from depleted soils increases siltation and contributes to agricultural nonpoint source pollution. Along with runoff water, contaminants such as pesticides, fertilizers, and field residues are carried into drinking water reservoirs and other surface waters.

Organic matter provides many benefits. Fertile soils rich in organic matter hold pesticides and fertilizers in place so crops can benefit from sensible applications. Soils rich in organic matter increase the availability of water to crops. In essence, compost acts as a water reservoir in the soil, increasing water-holding capacity and water retention.

With the steady reduction in farm numbers comes an increased need for a practical knowledge base, better training, and partnerships aimed at stewardship of the land. Consequently, several government agencies saw the need to provide easily accessible composting information to agricultural producers and others who compost organic byproducts.

This field guide is designed to bring practical composting information to the fingertips of agricultural producers and others who have an interest in composting. The *Field Guide to On-Farm Composting* was developed as a companion book to the popular NRAES publication, *On-Farm Composting Handbook*. This field guide contains firsthand problem-solving techniques that can be implemented in the field without time-consuming research. Practical solutions to on-site problems are provided to save valuable time.

Agricultural producers worldwide continue to struggle with the disappearance of highly productive cropland due to urbanization, greater governmental regulation, environmental pressures, and economic hardships. The world is getting smaller. We hope this publication will add one more tool for agricultural producers and other stewards of the land to remain competitive, productive, and independent.

Introduction

Composting can be defined as a managed biological oxidation process that converts heterogeneous organic matter into a more homogeneous, fine-particled, humus-like material. Throughout the composting process, organic matter is decomposed (first rapidly, then at a slower rate) until a stable organic mass is formed. In nature, decomposing organic materials are being stabilized or matured on a more or less continual basis. Compost maturity is important because it determines the usefulness of the compost as a soil amendment.

What Happens during Composting?

Composting begins as soon as appropriate materials are piled together. Initial mixing of raw materials introduces enough air to start the process. Almost immediately, microorganisms consume oxygen, and settling materials expel air from pore spaces. Aeration is provided either by passive air exchange or by forced aeration (using blowers and fans).

Temperature increases caused by microbial activity are noticeable within a few hours of pile formation. The temperature of composting materials usually increases rapidly to 120–140°F and remains in this range for several weeks. As active composting slows, temperatures gradually drop to 100°F and then to ambient air temperature.

A curing period usually follows the active composting stage. While curing, the materials continue to compost but at a much slower rate. The rate of oxygen consumption decreases to the point where the compost can be piled without turning or forced aeration.

The composting process does not stop at any particular point. Material continues to break down until the last remaining nutrients are consumed by the last remaining organisms and until nearly all carbon is converted to carbon dioxide. However, the compost becomes relatively stable and useful long before this point. Compost is judged to be "done" by characteristics related to its use and handling, such as carbon-to-nitrogen (C:N) ratio, oxygen demand, temperature, and odor (see "Process Evaluation," page 48).

Advantages of On-Farm Composting

Specific advantages of on-farm composting include:
- an efficient recycling method for crop residues and livestock mortalities;
- reduced moisture, weight, and volume of stored manure;
- reduced fly, weed, and odor problems in manures and other agricultural byproducts;
- a more stable form of nitrogen that is less likely to leach into water supplies; and
- a slower release of plant-available nutrients in the final product.

Using compost on the farm has a variety of agricultural and environmental benefits. On heavy soils, compost helps to reduce compaction and increases infiltration, which reduces erosion-causing runoff. By adding compost to soil on a regular basis, farmers maintain healthy soils and profitability. Many environmental agencies concerned with water quality are now encouraging recovery of organic byproducts in agriculture and food processing through on-farm composting.

Producing farm-generated compost and applying it to agricultural soils may be a part of more sustainable food production systems. Over 8,000 farms are now composting animal mortalities, manure, crop residues, and selected organic materials from communities and industries. At least 75% of farm composting operations are composting poultry mortalities (see chapter 5, "Composting Livestock and Poultry Mortalities," page 74).

The number of farm composters is expected to increase due to additional environmental restrictions, losses of available cropland, urban encroachment, the availability of suitable organic and nonagricultural byproducts, and a growing appreciation for the qualities and value of compost.

About This Guide

This guide is intended for use in the field. It is arranged into six chapters and designed to provide fast and easy access to information. In the back of the book are a case study regarding the benefits of compost use (appendix A), a table of metric conversions (appendix B), twenty-four color photographs (which are referenced throughout the text), and a list of references. Other highlights of the field guide include:

- an equipment identification table showing capacities and power requirements;
- diagrams showing windrow formation and shape;
- characteristics of commonly composted on-farm materials;
- a special section for first-time composters;
- tables and examples for recipe making, compost use estimation, and common laboratory conversions;
- a troubleshooting guide;
- calculations for sizing a compost pad;
- causes and control of odors, runoff, vectors, and dust;
- a chapter devoted to the composting of large and small livestock carcasses; and
- uses of compost on the farm and application rate calculations.

For more in-depth information about topics presented in this guide, refer to the *On-Farm Composting Handbook,* NRAES–54 (see references section for a complete citation). The *On-Farm Composting Handbook* also discusses topics not covered in this field guide, such as site selection and planning, economics, and marketing.

Overview of Composting Methods

There are at least five basic approaches to composting:

1. Passive or open-pile composting
2. Windrow composting using a loader for turning, mixing, and handling
3. Windrow composting using specialized windrow turners
4. Aerated static pile systems using perforated pipes
5. A variety of contained, or in-vessel, systems

All of these methods have been used successfully on farms. The first three methods usually take place outdoors. The last two methods, aerated static piles and in-vessel systems, are often covered or enclosed by a building, which allows for better moisture control and odor capture and treatment.

To a large degree, the physical and handling characteristics of the raw materials affect the type of composting method selected. Site sensitivity, distance to neighbors, cost, and speed of composting also affect the selection.

Passive or Open-Pile Composting

Open-pile composting is suitable for small to moderate-sized farms operating under a low level of management. This method involves forming piles of organic materials and leaving them undisturbed until the materials have decomposed into a stabilized product. Small piles are designed to take advantage of natural air movement. As an actively composting pile heats from the inside, the warm air rises, pulling cooler, fresher air inward from the sides and bottom (figure 1a). Depending on the looseness of the pile, wind currents can also move air through the pile. In general, larger piles are more difficult to aerate effectively because of pile compaction. Under proper feedstock and moisture conditions, however, these piles can get quite hot and produce good compost.

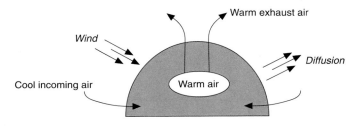

As an actively composting pile heats inside, the warm air rises, pulling cooler, fresher air inward from the sides and bottom.

FIGURE 1a. Natural (passive) air movement in a composting pile or windrow

To allow sufficient air exchange and heat release when composting manures with a high temperature potential (such as horse manure), do not allow the pile height to exceed about 3–4 feet. Keeping piles reasonably small (especially during warm conditions) helps dissipate excess heat.

The costs of the labor and equipment used to form and mix the initial piles are the largest operational expenses. Farm loaders and manure spreaders are usually briefly diverted from other farm uses to form and mix piles.

Passive or undisturbed composting is used in the livestock industry to compost animal carcasses (see chapter 5, "Composting Livestock and Poultry Mortalities," page 74). A disadvantage of passive composting is that if an unmanaged pile becomes too wet or compacted, it can quickly become anaerobic and very odorous.

Turned Windrows and Piles

This is the most common form of on-farm composting. Windrows and piles are agitated or turned to actively manage the process (figure 1b, page 4).

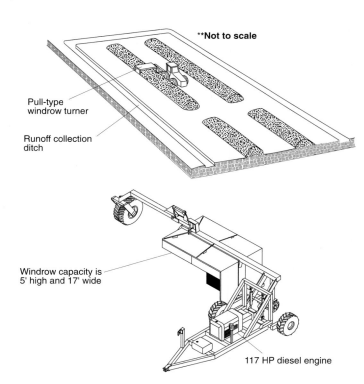

FIGURE 1b. Pull-type windrow turner in operation
Lower illustration adapted from Wildcat Manufacturing.

The most important effect of turning is rebuilding porosity to improve air exchange. Turning also exchanges material at the windrow surface with material from the interior. In this way, materials are composted evenly and weed seeds, pathogens, and fly larvae may be destroyed by the high interior temperatures. Turning further blends composting materials, breaks them into smaller particles, and increases their biologically active surface area. Excessive turning may reduce porosity if particle sizes become too small.

The equipment used for turning determines the size, shape, and spacing of individual windrows or piles. Depending on the size of the operation, either front-end loaders or special turning machines are used for windrow turning.

The Loader-Turned Windrow Approach (for Small to Moderate-Sized Operations)

No additional equipment or investment is required for the loader-turned windrow approach. Piles are turned with a tractor and bucket loader (photo 1a) or with a manure spreader and tractor-loader combination (photo 1b). Volumes of material can range from less than a hundred to several thousand cubic yards per year.

The Specialized-Equipment Approach (for Moderate-Sized to Large Operations)

Many farmers with expanding compost operations invest in specialized windrow turners (photo 1c). A small PTO-driven windrow turner (photo 1d) can process roughly 400 tons of material per hour. Larger windrow-turning machines, including self-propelled models, can process over 4,000 tons per hour. Additional labor may be required for maintenance and operation. A loader is still required for initial pile formation, pile maintenance, and other tasks such as feeding a compost screener or shredder.

Aerated Static Piles

Aerated static piles are closely managed piles or windrows that can be outside in the open or covered by a structure. Passively aerated static piles have open-ended perforated pipes embedded in each pile. As hot gases inside the pile rise, air is drawn into the pipes and up through the pile or windrow (photo 1e). Forced aeration takes the piped aeration system one step further, using a blower to supply air to the bottom of the composting pile (figure 1c). Alternatively, air can be drawn through the pile using negative or suction pressure. Forced-air systems generally provide more direct control of the compost process and permit larger piles. Negative pressure arrangements allow exhaust air to be directed through a biological filter if odor is a problem.

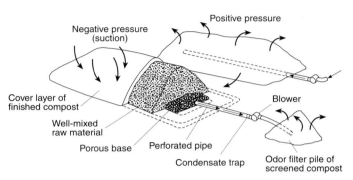

FIGURE 1c. Aerated static pile layout

Aerated static piles have a base of wood chips, chopped straw, or other porous material (figure 1c). The porous base material contains the perforated aeration pipe. Selection and initial mixing of raw materials are critical, because the pile must have a good structure to maintain porosity throughout the entire composting period. This generally requires a fairly stiff bulking agent such as straw or wood chips.

The initial height of an aerated static pile is 5–8 feet. In the winter, larger piles help retain heat. A layer of finished compost or bulking agent over the pile insulates the actively aerated pile from heat loss and maintains high temperatures in the outer pile layers for more complete pathogen destruction in manures. The top covering also helps protect the surface from drying and filters ammonia and other odors from the pile. The length of an aerated static pile is limited by air distribution in the aeration pipe. For more information regarding the design of forced aeration systems for farm composting, see the *On-Farm Composting Handbook* (NRAES–54).

In-Vessel Systems

In-vessel composting involves confining actively composting materials within a building, container, or vessel. In-vessel systems are the most aggressively managed and generally the most capital-intensive of the composting technologies. However, they also offer more control of the composting process. Most in-vessel methods rely on a variety of forced aeration and mechanical turning techniques to speed up the composting process. Some systems use containers to enclose composting materials without turning, such as the system shown in photo 1f.

Small in-vessel container systems that are insulated for year-round use are available for composting a variety of farm-generated organic materials, including poultry mortalities and manures. Many of these systems combine attributes of turned windrow and aerated static pile methods. Photo 1g shows an insulated rotating drum composter suitable for farm use.

For more information about in-vessel systems, see the *On-Farm Composting Handbook* (NRAES–54). The focus of this book will be on turned windrow and piles — the most common form of on-farm composting.

CHAPTER 1: Operations and Equipment

This chapter reviews basic operations and equipment needed for on-farm composting, including grinding, shredding, mixing, turning, curing, screening, blending, bagging, and storing. A table showing capacity and power requirements for diverse composting equipment is provided at the end of the chapter.

Feedstock Preparation

Most agricultural materials require little preparation for composting. However, some materials may need to be preprocessed by grinding, shredding, or sorting. Table 1-1 lists materials and equipment used for preparing compost feedstock.

TABLE 1-1. Materials and equipment used for preparing compost feedstock

Operation	Equipment
Material transfer	Front-end loader, dump truck, conveyor system
Particle size reduction	Chipper, grinder, hammermill, mixing drum, mower, paper shredder, shear shredder, tub grinder, windrow turner
Oxygen control	Blower, pipe, condensate trap (to protect the blower in a suction-type system)
pH control	Additives,[a] aeration system[b]
Biological reaction/mixing	Batch mixer, mixer/rotating mixing drum, pug mill, water-adding system, water truck

Adapted from *Composting for Municipalities: Planning and Design Considerations* (NRAES–94).

[a] Use of wet, high-nitrogen feedstocks, such as food residuals, apple and grape pomace, and waste potatoes, may require amendment with wood ash, kiln dust, lime mud, or other liming products to raise the initial pH of the mix. Compost feedstocks that have a high lime or alkaline content, such as some animal beddings, act to buffer a low-pH feedstock.

[b] Proper pile aeration maintains optimum oxygen conditions for aerobic activity. If aeration is insufficient at any point in the process, anaerobic conditions will develop and pH will drop to about 4.5, hindering the composting process. In most cases, aeration or turning can prevent anaerobic conditions from becoming so severe that pH falls below neutral (pH 7.0).

Mechanical and biological preparation of feedstock help establish the proper conditions for composting. Table 1-2 (page 8) shows the target conditions for active composting, including pile carbon-to-nitrogen (C:N) ratio, moisture content, oxygen concentration, particle size, porosity, bulk density, pH, and temperature. Although these are recommended targets for active composting, conditions outside these ranges may also yield successful results.

Grinding and Shredding

Certain raw materials such as tree stumps, branches, and other large compostables may require grinding and shredding. The most important effect of proper particle size reduction is to speed composting by increasing the available surface area of the material being

TABLE 1-2. Recommended conditions for active composting

Parameter	Target range [a]
Carbon-to-nitrogen (C:N) ratio	20:1–40:1 [b]
Moisture content	40–65% [c]
Oxygen concentration	> 5% [d]
Particle size (diameter in inches)	0.5–2
Pile porosity	> 40% [c]
Bulk density (lbs/cu yd)	800–1,200
pH	5.5–9.0
Temperature (°F)	110–150

Adapted from *On-Farm Composting Handbook* (NRAES–54).

[a] Although these recommendations are for active composting, conditions outside these ranges may also yield successful results.

[b] Weight basis (w:w). C:N ratios above 30 will minimize the potential for odors.

[c] Depends upon the specific materials, pile size, and/or weather conditions.

[d] An increasing likelihood of significant odors occurs at approximately 3% oxygen or less. Maintaining aerobic conditions is key to minimizing odors.

composted. Smaller particles expose more surface area to microbial activity.

Windrow turners provide some shredding of items such as paper and cardboard. However, high-speed turning machines, if overused, can physically destroy the porosity and texture of a compost mix. Excessive turning, grinding, or shredding may pulverize materials and should be avoided. If particle sizes are too small, piled materials will pack together and impede air movement.

The hammermill is the primary type of size-reduction equipment used in composting. Shear shredders and rotating drums are occasionally used. For wood, several types of chippers are available. Factors to consider in selecting a size-reducing device include (in order of importance):

1. Capital and operating costs (including power consumption)
2. Appropriateness in relation to feedstock characteristics and desired product
3. Capacity and speed
4. Safety
5. Compatibility with existing equipment
6. Maintenance requirements

Hammermills consist of rotating sets of fixed or swinging steel hammers through which raw material is fed. Hammer axles can be mounted either horizontally or vertically. The hammers break apart material until particles are small enough to drop through a discharge grate. Hammermills without an exit grate are sometimes referred to as flail mills. Hammermills can be very noisy.

A *tub grinder* is a specialized type of hammermill used primarily for woody materials. Tub grinders have a rotating tub intake system to feed the hammer chamber. As material is ground, it is forced through a screen or other restricted opening and then conveyed into standing piles or a transfer vehicle. Some grinders have grapples for loading, as shown in table 1-5, page 23 (illustration 3). Typically, a tub grinder requires two persons — one to operate the grinder and one to load materials into the machine. Some machines have remote control features.

Hammermills and tub grinders require regular maintenance, including rotation (balancing) and replacement of the hammers. Hammers typically need to be rotated after about 50 hours of operation and replaced after 140–200 hours of operation; however, these estimates vary considerably based on feedstock and equipment manufacturer. Hammers will wear more quickly if the steel surfaces are of poor quality or if there is a lot of abrasive material (such as sand and gravel) in the woody debris.

Shear shredders usually consist of a set of counter-rotating knives or hooked cutter discs (each several centimeters thick) that rotate at low speed and high torque. Rotating or rotary shear shredders draw material down toward the cutter shafts at the base of the hopper (table 1-5, page 23, illustration 1). The overlapping cutters slice or tear particles into smaller pieces until they pass through the spaces between the cutter discs. The tearing action of shear shredders can be used to enhance decomposition by opening up the internal structure of an organic feedstock. Many models can be trailer-mounted. Some manufacturers may use counteracting augers in place of cutting discs.

For yard trimmings with minor amounts of branches, smaller belt-type shear shredders can be used. These shredders can be either stationary or trailer-mounted and reduce the size of material through the action of a cleated belt (figure 1-1). Loose material is loaded into a receiving hopper, which feeds a conveyor. The conveyor drops the material onto the cleated belt that shreds the load by a continuous raking action. Material is shredded by being forced against stationary knives. Adjustable sweep fingers force oversized pieces back for further shredding, while materials such as sticks and stones are rejected and discharged through a trash chute.

Chippers and other grinders/shredders reduce particle sizes using various combinations of rotating and stationary cutters along with some form of restricted discharge opening (such as a bar grate or screen). Chippers slice particles using knives mounted on a cylinder or disc that rotates within a fixed housing.

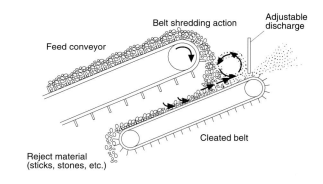

FIGURE 1-1. Belt-type shear shredder

!!CAUTION: Agricultural forage harvesters should not be used for shredding compost ingredients. They are not designed for hand feeding and have little or no safety provisions to protect the operator feeding the chopper.

Mixing and Pile Formation

Once a proper recipe has been selected (see "Recipe Making," page 34), feedstock ingredients are mixed to ensure rapid decomposition and quality compost. This is the start of active composting. One of the major benefits of mixing is to uniformly distribute nutrients and microorganisms throughout the composting pile.

For aerated static piles, mixing is critical because it is done only once. With turned windrows and piles, initial mixing blends raw materials to some degree of consistency. Subsequent turnings mix the material even more thoroughly. With most in-vessel technologies, mixing is incorporated into the composting process.

After mixing, the material is formed into a pile or windrow (photos 1-1 and 1-2) or loaded into a vessel. Since mixing and pile formation demand more labor than other composting operations, available bucket loaders, dump trucks, batch mixers, and other equipment are often used to reduce on-farm labor costs and improve efficiency, as described below.

Bucket loaders can perform almost all composting tasks, including mixing and pile/windrow formation (figure 1-2). Mixing is accomplished by repeatedly bucketing the ingredients together. For single-loader mixing, concrete buck walls with a concrete pad make mixing more efficient (figure 1-3, page 11).

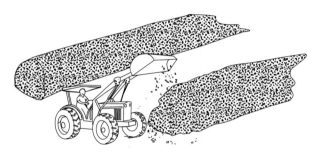

FIGURE 1-2. Mixing and pile formation with a bucket loader

Windrow dimensions should not be so large as to inhibit proper aeration and must conform to the capabilities of the turning equipment. If a specialized turner is used, a specific pile configuration may be required. Figures 1-4 (page 11) and 1-5 (page 12) present recommended windrow dimensions and spacing for various pile shapes. Table 1-3 (page 12) presents the approximate volume, in cubic yards per 100 feet of windrow, for pile shapes shown in figure 1-4.

If the composting site is some distance from the mixing area, dump trucks or wagons can be used to transport mixed ingredients to the site and build the initial pile or windrow (photo 1-3). Materials are often unloaded directly into windrows by backing up to the end of the existing windrow and tilting the bed of the truck or wagon while slowly moving the vehicle forward (figure 1-6, page 14). The speed and vehicle bed dimensions will determine the pile/windrow height. If necessary, a front-end loader can be used to reshape or enlarge the pile/windrow formed.

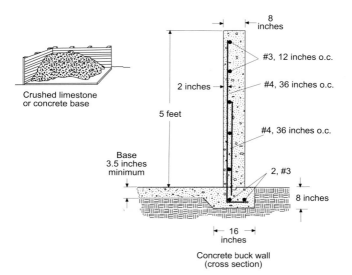

FIGURE 1-3. Buck wall design for mixing area

Source: Northeast Dairy Practices Council

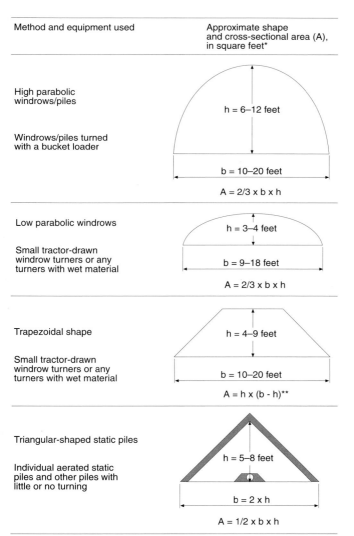

Method and equipment used	Approximate shape and cross-sectional area (A), in square feet*
High parabolic windrows/piles Windrows/piles turned with a bucket loader	h = 6–12 feet b = 10–20 feet A = 2/3 x b x h
Low parabolic windrows Small tractor-drawn windrow turners or any turners with wet material	h = 3–4 feet b = 9–18 feet A = 2/3 x b x h
Trapezoidal shape Small tractor-drawn windrow turners or any turners with wet material	h = 4–9 feet b = 10–20 feet A = h x (b - h)**
Triangular-shaped static piles Individual aerated static piles and other piles with little or no turning	h = 5–8 feet b = 2 x h A = 1/2 x b x h

* Volume (cubic yards) = [cross-sectional area (square feet) x length of windrow (feet)] ÷ 27 cubic feet/cubic yard

** This formula is an approximation and is valid only when the base is greater than or equal to twice the height.

FIGURE 1-4. Selected windrow shapes and dimensions

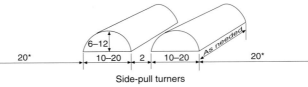
Side-pull turners

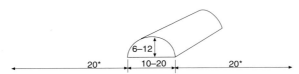
Bucket loader-turned windrows and piles

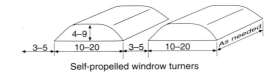
Self-propelled windrow turners

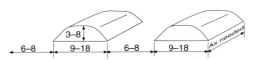
Tractor-assisted windrow turners (two-pass)

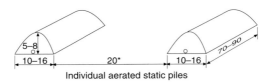
Individual aerated static piles

NOTE: Dimensions are in feet.
* Or enough space to maneuver loaders

FIGURE 1-5. Suggested windrow spacings

TABLE 1-3. Approximate volume, in cubic yards, per 100 feet of windrow

High parabolic windrows/piles – turned with bucket loader [a]

Base (feet)	Volume (cubic yards) Height (feet)						
	6	7	8	9	10	11	12
10	148	174	196	222	248	270	296
12	178	207	237	267	296	326	356
14	207	240	277	311	344	381	415
16	237	278	315	356	396	433	474
18	267	311	356	400	444	489	533
20	296	344	396	444	493	544	593

[a] Volume = (2/3 base x height x 100 feet) ÷ 27 cubic feet/cubic yard

(continued on next page)

TABLE 1-3. Approximate volume, in cubic yards, per 100 feet of windrow *(continued)*

Triangular-shaped static piles [b]

Base (feet)	Volume (cubic yards) Height (feet)					
	5	6	7	8	9	10
10	93	111	130	148	167	185
12	111	133	156	178	200	222
14	130	156	181	207	233	259
16	148	178	207	237	267	296
18	167	200	233	267	300	333

[b] Volume = (1/2 base x height x 100 feet) ÷ 27 cubic feet/cubic yard

Trapezoidal shape — most windrow turners [c]

Base (feet)	Volume (cubic yards) Height (feet)					
	4	5	6	7	8	9
10	89	93	—	—	—	—
11	104	111	—	—	—	—
12	119	130	133	—	—	—
13	133	148	156	—	—	—
14	148	167	178	181	—	—
15	163	185	200	207	—	—
16	178	204	222	233	237	—
17	193	222	244	259	267	—
18	207	241	267	285	296	300
19	222	259	289	311	326	333
20	237	278	311	337	356	367

[c] Volume = [height (base − height) x 100 feet] ÷ 27 cubic feet/cubic yard *(Note: This formula is an approximation and is valid only when the base is greater than or equal to twice the height.)*

Low parabolic windrows — passively aerated windrows, small windrow turners, or wet materials [d]

Base (feet)	Volume (cubic yards) Height (feet)				
	3	3.5	4	4.5	5
9	67	78	89	100	111
10	74	85	100	111	122
11	81	96	107	122	137
12	89	104	119	133	148
13	96	111	130	144	159
14	104	122	137	156	174

[d] Volume = (2/3 base x height x 100 feet) ÷ 27 cubic feet/cubic yard

NOTE: Shapes are illustrated in figure 1-4, page 11. Volumes in this table are for use in estimating the volume of raw materials in a windrow or pile. The cover and base material are not accounted for. If a base or insulating cover is used, consider it when estimating the space required for the pile.

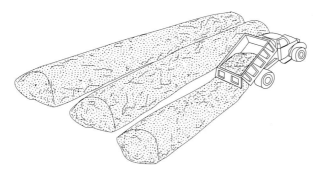

FIGURE 1-6. Dump truck used to form windrows

Batch mixers similar to those used to mix livestock feed are effective for many feedstock materials. Several types of batch mixers have been used and tested for composting operations, including mixers with augers, rotating paddles, and slats on a continuous chain. Most batch mixers can be truck- or wagon-mounted and, if equipped with sizable loading hoppers, can eliminate the need for dump trucks or wagons. Manure spreaders, especially side-delivery, flail-type spreaders, can be used to mix feedstock and form windrows (figure 1-7).

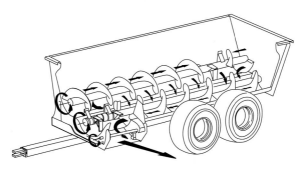

Cut-away view showing material flow

FIGURE 1-7. Side-delivery, flail-type manure spreader
Reprinted with permission from Knight Manufacturing Corporation, Brodhead, Wisconsin

Depending on the wetness of the feedstock ingredients being mixed, the mixing mechanism in a batch mixer should not be operated too long (perhaps only a few minutes), otherwise free airspace created by the bulking agent may become filled with the wetter feedstock, which decreases porosity. Another common failure of batch mixers is that long straw or similar fibers are not easily handled by the mixing mechanism. Drier bulking agents or amendments are generally placed into a batch mixer first, then more dense, wetter materials are added on top.

Two other pieces of equipment available to mix and homogenize piles are stationary pug mills and rotating drum mixers. Stationary pug mills use slowly counter-rotating paddles or hammers to blend materials and produce a good mix on a continuous basis (table 1-5, page 23, illustration 6). Pug mills are faster than batch-operated mixers, but feedstock must be fed into pug mills continuously in the proper proportions. Also, pug mills lack the mobility provided by batch mixers.

Rotating drum mixers (table 1-5, page 23, illustration 5) have also been used for blending compost feedstock. Residence times can vary from a few hours to several days, depending on the drum length, diameter, material depth, and rotation speed. Some of the larger rotating drums hold feedstock for up to 36 hours and serve as first-stage biological reactors.

Active Composting

During active composting, readily available nutrient and energy sources are transformed into carbon dioxide, heat, water, and compost (figure 1-8). Given adequate time and environmental conditions, most components of a farm's organic byproducts are readily compostable (see table 2-1, page 27).

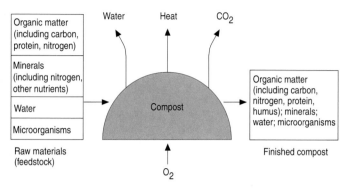

The carbon, protein, and water in the finished compost is less than that in the raw materials. The finished compost has more humus. The volume of the finished compost is 50% or less of the volume of raw material.

FIGURE 1-8. Aerobic composting

After a pile or windrow is formed, pile porosity and aeration become the critical factors for preventing odor formation. Proper nutrient balance, particle size, moisture content, temperature, and bulk density are also necessary for optimum pile performance and odor reduction. For specific recommendations regarding odor management, see "Odor Control," page 62.

In an actively managed compost pile, turning either with a bucket loader (figure 1-2, page 10) or a windrow turner (figure 1b, page 4) is done periodically to fluff up the pile and enhance pile aeration (see sidebar, page 16). If certain time and temperature conditions are achieved, existing pathogens and other noxious substances are controlled. Subsequent curing, screening, storing, and packaging operations further prepare the compost for a variety of end uses. For a description of the active composting process, including management and troubleshooting, see chapter 3, "Process Control and Evaluation," beginning on page 44.

Compost Curing

Curing is the last stage of the composting process that occurs after most of the organic feedstock material has been decomposed and stabilized. Curing provides maturity, which means the energy and nutrient-containing materials in the compost have been transformed into a stable organic mass. A mature compost has undergone decomposition, contains slowly releasing plant nutrients, is low in phytotoxins (plant-harmful substances), and no longer ties up large amounts of nitrogen and oxygen when mixed with soil. One of the most reliable indications that curing should begin is a sustainable drop in the temperature of a well-managed, actively composting pile (see sidebar, page 17).

In general, turned windrow compost operations producing less than 500 cubic yards of compost per year will do fine using conventional front-end loaders. Facilities producing between 500 and 2,000 cubic yards of compost per year may need at least a small windrow turner. Large operations (more than 2,000 cubic yards per year) will require additional mixing and grinding equipment, along with a turner for more efficient material handling.

While larger municipal-type front-end loaders (135-horsepower, with a 3-yard bucket) take about one minute to go through a single load/dump cycle, farm loaders are capable of similar performance. The amount of material loaders can process per hour is proportional to the size of their buckets. Thus, a farmer can increase the turning rate ninefold by using a 3-yard bucket loader in place of a ⅓-yard loader. However, the capital cost of a 3-yard municipal-type loader is roughly nine times that of a skid loader or small tractor with a ⅓-yard bucket loader.

In general, turning becomes less costly on a per-unit basis and windrow turners become more cost-efficient as the volume of material increases. Small skid loaders (40-horsepower, with a ⅓-yard bucket) and tractor loaders (85-horsepower, with a 1-yard bucket) offer the most cost-effective turning at small volumes and remain relatively inexpensive even as volumes increase. For small-scale windrow turning, existing farm loaders can be equipped with hydraulically operated augers (see figure at right).

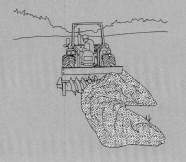

If immature compost is stored without sufficient aeration, undesirable odors can result. If applied to a growing medium, immature compost may interfere with plant growth by immobilizing nitrogen and causing ammonia toxicity or by causing oxygen deficiency in planted soils. Compost used for plant potting media must be more stable or mature than compost destined for mixing with soil. For information on how to determine the level of maturity in a finished compost, see "Sampling and Laboratory Testing," page 48.

During curing, clumps and air channels that may have formed during active composting should be broken up. Moisture levels should be maintained above 45–50% by turning, mixing, and adding make-up liquids, as necessary. However, if a low-moisture product is required for bagging or spreading, be careful not to add too much water since little additional drying occurs during curing.

A primary management concern during curing is prevention of high temperatures or anaerobic conditions. Curing piles must be small enough to permit natural aeration and should be monitored for temperature and odor. In curing piles that are odorous or actively heating, forced aeration or reduced pile size may be recommended.

!!CAUTION: In large, woody piles, moisture content, temperature, and particle size should be monitored and controlled due to the risk of fire (see "Fires," page 72).

WHEN IS COMPOST READY FOR CURING?

In a well-managed windrow, the failure of compost to reheat after turning is an indication that it is ready for curing (see figure below). At this stage, biological activity in the pile has slowed enough to allow the compost to be cured in piles or windrows for long periods of time without significant handling. If the composting process has been managed correctly, the material should be pathogen-safe and inoffensive. Curing provides additional time to further stabilize the material and decompose odorous organic acids and phytotoxins that may have been generated during initial composting.

Actively composting piles may be ready for curing in as little as three weeks; however, three months is more typical, and longer times are possible. Care must be taken that decreased temperatures in the active pile or windrow are not a result of process limitations, such as inadequate or excessive moisture. To see if this is the case, thoroughly wet a small sample of the compost, seal it in a plastic bag, and store the bag at room temperature (68–86°F). If the compost does not emit a foul odor after one week in the bag, it can be considered stable enough for curing. Curing piles are maintained for as long as necessary to achieve the desired level of compost stability. Consequently, curing times may range from several weeks to as long as eight months or more.

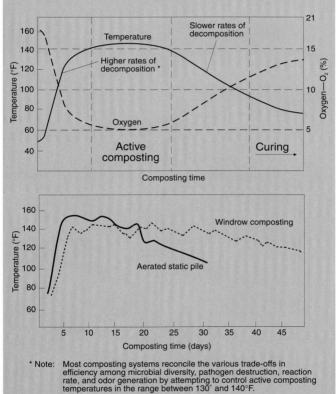

* Note: Most composting systems reconcile the various trade-offs in efficiency among microbial diversity, pathogen destruction, reaction rate, and odor generation by attempting to control active composting temperatures in the range between 130° and 140°F.

Time–temperature–oxygen patterns for composting; general (top) and typical (bottom)

Screening

Screening separates materials of different sizes, shapes, and weights and can improve compost quality by removing

- oversized materials,
- clumps of compost,
- small inerts, and
- unwanted material that is not fully composted.

Larger organic particles that are screened out after curing can be recycled back to the feedstock preparation step. If screening is delayed until after curing, larger particles will continue to maintain pile porosity in the curing piles. Also, screened compost that is stored too long may develop clumps that can reduce its usefulness. If necessary, screening can be followed by refining operations to remove small inert pieces such as glass, metal fragments, plastic bits, and film plastics. Most on-farm composters do not perform refining operations, however, since farm-generated feedstocks are relatively free of small inerts. Table 1-4 presents a list of equipment available for screening and refining operations.

TABLE 1-4. Equipment for screening and refining operations

Operation	Equipment
Screening	Auger and trough screen, disc screen (scalping disc), flexing belt screen, power screen, rotary screen (spinning disc), shaker screen, trommel with discharge conveyor, vibrating screen
Refining [a]	Ballistic (cyclone) separator, dust collection system, destoner/fluidized bed separator (air classifier)
Size reduction	Hammermill, shredder

Adapted from *Composting for Municipalities: Planning and Design Considerations* (NRAES–94) and *On-Farm Composting Handbook* (NRAES–54).

[a] Refining technologies shown in this table are informational only. Most on-farm composters do not require such a high level of material separation, since farm-generated feedstocks are relatively free of small pieces of glass, metal fragments, plastic bits, and film plastics.

Prior to screening, compost may need to be moistened with water sprays to minimize dust generation. Excessive dust should be controlled because it can

- create a nuisance,
- potentially impede operations,
- decrease machine efficiency, and
- affect operator health.

Care must be used when adding water to control dust, as excessive moisture can reduce screen efficiency. The proper moisture content for compost screening is generally between 35% and 45%, depending on the type of screen used . For management methods to control dust on site, see "Dust Control," page 70.

Four generic types of screens are available: stationary, vibrating, disc, and rotating or trommel. When selecting screens, important characteristics to consider include:

- screen opening size and types,
- capacity (throughput),
- cost,
- compatibility with existing equipment,
- effectiveness in providing the desired level of separation, and
- susceptibility to blinding (that is, clogging or blockage of screen openings).

For screening compost, screen openings should be ¼–½ inch, depending upon the material being separated and the end use of the compost. Smaller openings reduce the output of the screen and increase the risk of blinding.

A *trommel screen* is a rotating screen that often includes a feed hopper and loading conveyor (table 1-5, page 25, illustration 8). The drum is inclined or contains internal flights to move the material through as it rotates. Larger particles are retained within the drum, while fine particles fall through the holes onto a conveyor or base pad. Some trommel screens have a segment of the screen surface exposed at the top of its revolution where a rotary brush can be mounted to clear screen openings and prevent blinding. Photo 1-4 shows a homemade trommel screen.

A *shaker screen* creates a reciprocating motion that bounces material along the length of the screen. The shaking motion helps separate large and small particles, reduces blinding, and helps move oversized particles off the screen. Shaker screens are consolidated into a single unit consisting of a feed hopper, conveyor, and screen. Screens are either wire-mesh-type, perforated panels or "piano wire" screens. Often, several levels of screens are stacked to separate materials into several size ranges. Shaker screens may include cleaning balls that dislodge material blinding the screen openings.

A *vibrating screen* also uses an oscillating or reciprocating motion to enhance separation. However, the vibrating action is much faster than that of a shaker screen. Vibration and the slope of the screen act to move oversized particles. This type of screen also uses wire mesh screens, multiple decks of screens, and cleaning balls (or rings). Illustration 9 in table 1-5 on page 25 shows a portable vibrating screen being loaded with a backhoe.

A *flexing belt screen* comes in at least two different designs. One type uses a very durable slotted belt that is alternately flexed and snapped to throw material up into the air. Another type uses a perforated belt that moves in a wavelike pattern. The resulting motion bounces material up and down as it travels along the screen.

A *disc screen* or *scalping disc* uses banks of overlapping, scalloped-edged rotating discs to move coarse items from one end of the screen to the other. Smaller pieces fall between the discs as they rotate. Scalping discs are designed to remove large items and may therefore serve as the first stage in a screening system that includes several other screens and shredders.

An *auger* or *trough screen* consists of a perforated trough containing an auger that moves materials from one end to the other. Fine materials drop through the holes, and coarser materials pass through to the end. Multiple auger screens can be combined to achieve multiple separations of particle sizes, including the removal of soil and fine materials from wood chips.

A *rotary screen* or *spinning disc* has plates or discs with holes of a selected size onto which material is fed. The spinning action separates material by throwing oversize material to the outside. Rotary screens are often used in sawmills to separate sawdust from larger materials.

Storing and Packaging

Storage is normally the last step in the compost process before final use. Storage is needed to accommodate the time between when compost is ready and when it is used. For a typical farm, three or more months of compost production may need to be stored on site (depending on field and pasture management).

Stored, stable compost can be piled higher than either active or curing piles. However, if piles are stored wet, anaerobic conditions remain a risk. Finished compost that has been properly composted and cured still has a low ongoing rate of microbial activity. Stored piles should not be ignored and must be managed to avoid potential pathogen recontamination, weed contamination, and fire hazards.

Pathogen and weed contamination during storage of compost can be avoided by protecting the storage area from animals such as birds. Fleece or other breathable covers can be used to protect outdoor storage piles. It is also good practice to restack compost from large storage piles into smaller piles a few weeks prior to use. This allows stored compost to aerate naturally and dissipates any phytotoxic compounds that may be present.

The height and width of stored compost piles are generally determined by the reach of available loaders, conveyors, or other materials handling equipment (figure 1-9). However, as stored pile height increases above 12 feet, the risk of spontaneous combustion in the pile increases. Periodic temperature monitoring of stored piles can signal the need for turning in an incompletely stabilized (actively heating) compost. All compost storage areas should be well drained, with surface runoff channeled away from the piles. Open-sided buildings (figure 1-10) are ideal for storing finished compost. Photo 1-5 shows a commodity-type storage shed being used for compost storage.

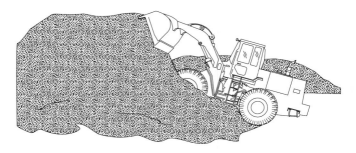

FIGURE 1-9. Moving stored compost with a bucket loader

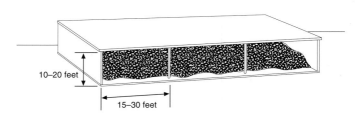

FIGURE 1-10. Open-sided storage for finished compost

Blending Amendments

Many composters across the United States are expanding compost sales by blending finished compost for retail sale. Existing screening equipment can often be equipped with shredders and mixers for blending. Mixing and blending equipment is used to add fertilizers or blend amendments such as sand to produce a topsoil.

In general, compost blends have the following characteristics:

- have predictable and uniform characteristics (to meet specific application requirements),
- contain other, more expensive ingredients (such as specific nutrients or trace elements), and
- command a relatively high sales price.

Blending is most often used to improve the physical characteristics and increase the organic matter content of a marketed topsoil. Specialized compost blends for nursery, golf course, and landscape applications have been successfully marketed throughout the United States. Typically, these compost blends are prepared for specific applications, often following the user's mixing instructions.

Bagging

Bagged compost brings a higher price than compost sold in bulk. Bagging is practiced only when the sales volume justifies the equipment and labor costs. High-volume bagging equipment includes hoppers with metered valves, scales, bag sealers, and one or more conveyors. If buyers require bags to be placed on pallets and wrapped, a pallet wrapper may be necessary. As long as it is cured and dried, compost that is bagged and pallet-wrapped can be stored on site. If desired, the entire bagging operation can be contracted to an independent vendor. Many composters provide on-site bag-your-own options to customers. For smaller operations, inexpensive, low-volume bagging equipment is available.

Bagging compost requires a very stable product, packaged at a moisture content of around 40–45%. Generally, a smaller screen size (⅜ inch or less) is desired for bagging. Since compost is continuously respiring if not dried out, it is best to delay bagging until the compost is ready to be shipped. The need for bagging should be evaluated by taking into consideration the following factors:

- labor and bagging equipment costs,
- potential compost selling price,
- market channels, and
- quality of bagged product.

Table 1-5 on pages 22–25 presents equipment throughput capacity and horsepower ranges for selected composting operations, including grinding/shredding, windrow turning, mixing, and screening.

TABLE 1-5. Selected compost equipment: available capacity and horsepower ranges

Type and description	Approximate capacity		Power
	Cubic yards per hour	(Tons per hour)	Horsepower
GRINDING/SHREDDING EQUIPMENT			
Hand-fed chipper (disc-type)	5–6" maximum diameter of materials		20–30
Hand-fed chipper (disc-type)	9–12" maximum diameter of materials		35–120
Hammermill	8–450	(4–225)	30–900
Paper and wood shredder	1–30	(0.5–15)	2–100
Rotary auger with counterknife	2–130	(1–65)	22–335
❶ Rotary shear shredder	0.4–200	(0.2–100)	7.5–600
❷ Shear shredder (belt-type)	10–250	(5–125)	5–110
Shredder with knives fixed to set of rotating disks	4–12	(2–6)	30–60
❸ Tub grinder	20–200	(10–100)	80–990
Vertical grinder	8–50	(4–25)	100–400
Vertical grinder – large capacity	100–450	(50–225)	1,000–2,000
Whole-tree chopper – disc-type (towed or self-propelled)	12–17" maximum diameter of materials		170–250
Whole-tree chopper – disc-type (towed or self-propelled)	19" maximum diameter of materials		400–500
Wood chipper – cutting disc-type	6–9" maximum diameter of materials		20–40
MIXING EQUIPMENT			
❹ Batch mixer – auger-type (10–30-cubic-yard capacity while mixing)	40–100	(20–50)	75–165
Batch mixer – reel-type (4–18-cubic-yard capacity while mixing)	–	–	10–50
❺ Rotating drum mixer	12–160	(6–80)	–
❻ Continuous mix pug mill	2–1,000	(1–500)	10–100

Note: Numbers along left-hand side of table correspond to numbers on illustrations on page 23. Equipment capacities vary considerably with materials, specific application, and optional equipment.

(continued on page 24)

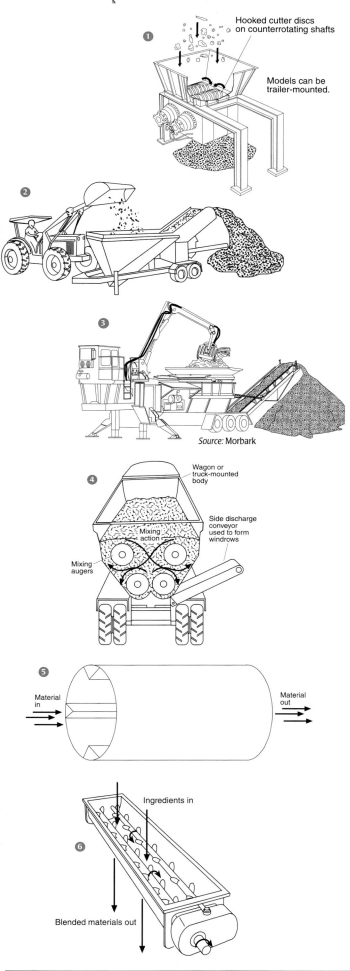

❶ Hooked cutter discs on counterrotating shafts

Models can be trailer-mounted.

❷

❸ *Source:* Morbark

❹ Wagon or truck-mounted body

Side discharge conveyor used to form windrows

Mixing action

Mixing augers

❺ Material in

Material out

❻ Ingredients in

Blended materials out

TABLE 1-5. Selected compost equipment: available capacity and horsepower ranges *(continued)*

Type and description	Approximate capacity		Power
	Cubic yards per hour	(Tons per hour)	Horsepower
WINDROW-TURNING EQUIPMENT			
❶ Aerator-composter (PTO-powered, rear-hitch-mounted to 60–130 hp tractor)	400–2,400	(200–1,200)	Tractor PTO
❷ Aerator-auger (mounted on front of 40–130 hp tractor)	–	–	Hydraulics
Auger-style turner (self-powered, self-propelled)	2,000–40,000	(1,000–20,000)	115–300
❸ Elevated face turner (self-powered, towed by 40–100 hp tractor)	3,000–4,000	(1,000–3,000)	65–85
Elevated face turner (self-powered, self-propelled)	2,000–6,000	(1,000–3,000)	100–150
❹ Rotary drum turner (ground-driven, towed by 35–70 hp tractor)	1,200–1,800	(600–900)	–
❺ Rotary drum turner (self-powered, self-propelled)	1,600–8,000	(800–4,000)	65–440
❻ Rotary drum turner (PTO-powered, towed by 60–140 hp tractor)	400–1,000	(200–500)	Tractor PTO
❼ Rotary drum turner (self-powered, towed by 70 hp tractor)	1,800–2,200	(900–1,100)	90–125
Rotary drum turner (self-powered, mounted on 3-cubic-yard front-end loader)	1,800–2,200	(900–1,100)	170–190
Rotary drum turner (self-powered, mounted on 4-cubic-yard front-end loader)	5,000	(2,500)	325
SCREENING EQUIPMENT			
Disc screen	20–80	(10–40)	–
Flexible belt screen	30–200	(15–100)	–
Oscillating (shaker) screen	Variable	–	–
❽ Trommel screen	20–150+	(10–75+)	–
❾ Vibrating screen	50–150+	(25–75+)	–

Note: Numbers along left-hand side of table correspond to numbers on illustrations on page 25. Equipment capacities vary considerably with materials, specific application, and optional equipment.

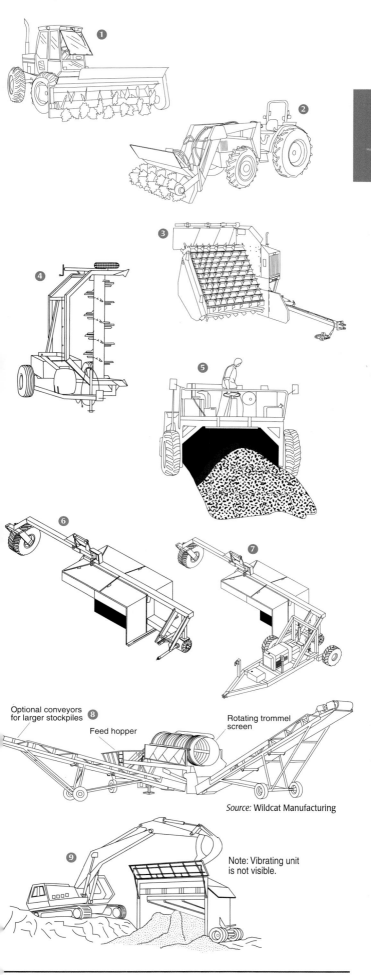

Optional conveyors
for larger stockpiles

Feed hopper

Rotating trommel
screen

Source: Wildcat Manufacturing

Note: Vibrating unit
is not visible.

CHAPTER 2: Raw Materials and Recipe Making

This chapter presents a brief description of the most common raw materials used for on-farm composting. A special section, "Advice for First-Time Composters," is also included. Easy-to-read tables and standard formulas are provided to assist in making a compost recipe. At the end of the chapter, a table of commonly used raw materials and their characteristics is presented.

Raw Materials

On many farms, the basic composting ingredients are manure generated on the farm and bedding. Straw (photo 2-1) and sawdust are common bedding materials. Nontraditional bedding materials are also used, including newspaper and chopped cardboard. Many farmers add other on-farm residues such as unusable hay and vegetables, corn cobs, cotton gin trash, and poultry mortalities. Photos 2-2 through 2-4 show several other types of farm-generated byproducts.

A wide variety of off-farm materials is used for on-farm composting, including paper and wood industry residues, horse manure (from private stables and racetracks), leaves, grass clippings, food processing and restaurant byproducts, discarded gypsum board, and municipal sludges (biosolids). Liquid byproducts such as beer, orange juice, and soda can also be used in the composting process. Organic materials from industrialized processes can be composted but require more caution than farm-generated ingredients. Producers interested in accepting off-farm materials should first check state or provincial environmental regulatory requirements regarding on-farm composting of these materials.

Table 2-1 (page 27) presents a variety of feedstocks and their general suitability for composting. Table 2-5 at the end of this chapter (page 43) provides typical percent nitrogen (dry weight), carbon-to-nitrogen (C:N) ratio, moisture content, and bulk density ranges for raw materials commonly used for on-farm composting.

Manure as a Composting Material

The amount of manure composted on a livestock farm is often determined by cleaning schedules, land availability, and weather conditions. For example, many dairy farmers compost only a selected portion of manure, such as the bedded-pack manure or the manure collected during dry weather. A number of dairy farmers compost solids that have been separated from liquid manure. Some use these separated solids for bedding without composting them.

Each type of manure has its own physical, chemical, and biological characteristics. Cattle and horse manures, when mixed with bedding, possess good qualities for composting (see table 2-1). Swine manure, which is very wet and usually not mixed with bedding material, needs to be mixed with straw or similar raw materials (see "Bulking Materials," page 31). Poultry manure also needs to be blended with carbonaceous materials — preferably those low in nitrogen, such as sawdust or straw. In general, the rapid decomposition and elevated temperatures of composting produce a manure byproduct that is relatively odor-free, easily handled, homogeneous, and biologically stable.

TABLE 2-1. Type and value of raw ingredients

Origin	C:N ratio, nutri-ents	Structure, porosity	Moisture –as is	Degrad-ability	Treatment required	Cau-tions
AGRICULTURAL RESIDUALS						
Poultry manure (fresh, no litter)	10	Poor	Moist	Good	Bulking material	Odor
Poultry manure (with litter)	13–30	Medium	Low-dry	Medium	–	Odor
Slurry (urine) liquid	2–3	Poor	Liquid	Good	Mix with dry matter	Odor
Manure (cattle) liquid	8–13	Poor	Liquid	Good	Mix with dry matter	Odor
Manure (pig)	5–7	Poor	High	Good	–	Odor, mois-ture
Cattle manure	20	Medium	Medium	High	–	–
Manure with straw	25–30	Good	Good	Medium	–	–
Horse manure	25	Good	Good	Medium	–	–
Vegetable wastes	13	Poor	Moist	High	–	Low pH, odor
Straw:						
–Oat/rye	60	Good	Dry	Medium	Rough chopping	–
–Wheat	100	Good	Dry	Medium	Rough chopping	–
–Barley/ pulses	40–50	Good	Dry	High	–	–
WOOD AND LUMBER INDUSTRY MATERIALS						
Bark	100–300; low P, Ca; low pH	Very good	Medium; good	Very good	Pre-grind	–
Paper sludge	100–110	Medium to poor	Very moist	Medium	Presscake	Dioxins
Cotton sludge	20–40; N-rich; low P, K	Poor	Very moist	Very good	Pressed	–
Sawdust:						
–Beech	~100	Very good	≤50%; good	Excellent	Already ground	–
–Fir	~230	Very good	≤50%; good	Medium	Already ground	–
–Aged	<100	Very good	≤50%; good	Poor	Already ground	–

(continued on next page)

TABLE 2-1. Type and value of raw ingredients *(continued)*

Origin	C:N ratio, nutrients	Structure, porosity	Moisture —as is	Degradability	Treatment required	Cautions
WOOD AND LUMBER INDUSTRY MATERIALS *(continued)*						
Cardboard	200–500	Medium to poor	Very low	Very good	Shred	Boron, colors
Wood ash [a]	n/a; K-Ca-rich; high in heavy metals	Poor	Very low	None	None	Metals, high pH
FRUIT PRESSING RESIDUES						
Grapes	Poor in P, Ca	Poor/ medium	Medium	Medium to low	Lime addition	Low pH, seed residues
Fruits	Poor in P, Ca	Poor	Medium	Fair to good	Lime addition	Low pH
GARDEN/LANDSCAPE MATERIALS						
Wood chips	40–100	Good	Too dry	Low	Grinding	Coarseness
Garden wastes	20–60	Good	Medium	Medium	Grinding	–
Green foliage	30–60	Medium to good	Good/ dry	Good	–	–
Leaves	–	Good	–	–	–	Matting
Grass clippings	12–25	Poor	Moist	High	Bulking material, pre-drying	Odor
Reeds/swamp matter	20–50	Good	Dry	Medium	Grinding	Coarseness
Ditch scrapings	10–15	Poor	Moist	Medium	Occasionally pressing	Salts/ lead on road-sides
OTHERS						
Peat (dark)	60–80	Good	Medium	Very low	–	Low pH
Peat (light)	60–80	Good	Medium	Low	–	Low pH
Slaughter wastes	15–18	Poor	Moist	High	–	Odor
Mushroom compost	40	Good	Good	Good/ medium	–	–

(continued on next page)

TABLE 2-1. Type and value of raw ingredients *(continued)*

Origin	C:N ratio, nutrients	Structure, porosity	Moisture –as is	Degradability	Treatment required	Cautions
OTHERS *(continued)*						
Rock powders [b]	Ca, K, Mg, trace elements	Poor	None	None	–	–
MSW [c]	30–120	Medium to poor	Very low	Medium	Grinding, moisture	Metals, glass, etc.
Biosolids (sewage sludge)	< 20; high P, N; low K; metals	Poor	High	Very good	Needs bulking material	Pathogens, metals
Food scraps	< 25; high K, salt	Very poor	High	Very high	Bulking material	Pathogens, salt
Coffee grounds	–	Medium	Medium to high	Medium	–	–

Source: Brinton, 1995.

[a] Used as additive to raise the pH in acidic feedstocks (pH < 5.0)

[b] Used as additive for mineral addition

[c] MSW (municipal solid waste) is waste material from residential, commercial, institutional, and industrial sources within a community. According to the U.S. Environmental Protection Agency, MSW does not include wastes from sources such as construction and demolition debris, automobile bodies, municipal sewage sludge (biosolids), combustion ash, and agricultural and industrial processes, or other wastes that might be disposed of in incinerators or landfills. For more information about MSW composting, see *Composting for Municipalities: Planning and Design Considerations* (NRAES–94), 1998.

Although manure composting is not yet a mainstream practice, it currently fills a niche where manure handling problems or excess nutrient balances occur. Composting also fits well on farms having a philosophy that encourages the recycling of manure as a soil-building resource. Given these reasons, the number of farms composting manure is likely to increase. See the sidebar on page 30 for more discussion of the reasons for composting manure. Table 2-2 on page 30 lists the production and characteristics of various types of fresh manure.

Advice for First-Time Composters

Many composters do a good job of combining raw materials by trial and error, by the "look and feel" of the mix, or by using whatever organic materials are available. This method is not recommended unless you already have experience (or have the help of someone with experience) using a particular feedstock/compost mix. If you are new to composting or are planning to use unfamiliar materials, use laboratory testing of raw materials along with standard methods to formulate a good compost mix. Following is some additional advice that can help ensure a successful compost recipe for the first-time composter.

TABLE 2-2. Production and characteristics of fresh manure (as produced with no bedding or water added)

| Animal | Animal weight (pounds) | Total manure production per animal per day | | Moisture content (%) | Density (pounds per cubic yard) |
		Pounds	Cubic feet[a]		
Beef cattle	750	45	0.75	85.3	1,700
Beef cattle	1,250	75	1.20	85.3	1,700
Dairy cattle	500	41	0.66	87.3	1,670
Dairy cattle	1,400	115	1.85	86.0	1,670
Veal	240[b]	15	0.24	91.6	1,670
Horse	1,000	45	0.75	70.6	1,700
Poultry					
Broilers	2	0.14	0.0024	74.1	1,700
Layers	4	0.21	0.0035	75.0	1,620
Sheep	100	4.0	0.062	72.5	1,730
Swine, finishing pig	150	9.8	2.2	90.8	1,620

Adapted from *Livestock Waste Facilities Handbook,* MWPS–18, 2nd edition, 1985.

Note: Values are approximate. The actual characteristics of a manure can easily have values 20% or more above or below the table values. The volume of waste that a waste-handling system has to handle can be much larger than the table values because of the addition of water, bedding, and so on.

[a] 1 cubic foot per day equals 13.5 cubic yards per year

[b] Average animal weight

Balancing Moisture Content and C:N Ratio

Developing an effective compost recipe means keeping the moisture content, C:N ratio, and other conditions of the mix within the recommended ranges shown in table 1-2 (page 8). A high moisture content (> 60%) yields anaerobic conditions that may lead to odors, delayed pile heating, and unwanted seepage. The consequences of a poor C:N ratio are somewhat less troublesome. Therefore, for wetter feedstock it is usually best to develop a recipe based on moisture content and then adjust the recipe to achieve an acceptable C:N ratio.

With drier feedstocks, the initial recipe can be developed on the basis of the C:N ratio, since it is relatively easy to add water or liquid feedstocks to a mix. When using this method, formulate the recipe using the two ingredients having the most extreme C:N ratios, then add other materials as available or needed. Note that the carbon availability in raw materials varies, depending on the surface area (determined by particle size) and extent of lignification of the material. Lignin, because of its complex structure and variety of chemical bonds, is resistant to decay. Consequently, the carbon in large wood chips is less available than the carbon in straw, even though their C:N ratios are similar.

The Importance of Porosity

Porosity is critical, because it determines how well air can enter and diffuse into the composting mass. Porosity, along with moisture content, is very closely related to aeration. If a compost recipe results in a mix with excessive moisture and/or poor porosity, reduced air diffusion in the pile will cause anaerobic, putrefying conditions, which lead to bad odors.

Excessive moisture occupies pore space, which in turn impedes air circulation to and from respiring organisms. Excessive moisture also makes materials heavy, causing them to collapse and compact under their own weight. Proper moisture content balances the need for both water- and air-filled pore space. The negative impact of a high-moisture feedstock such as a manure slurry can be offset in part by setting a high initial pile porosity with bulking materials (to help ensure free airspace in the pile). Pile bulk density is considered to be a good field indicator of potential airspace within a pile (see "Bulking Materials" below).

Bulking Materials

An ample supply of bulking materials is important, especially when composting large quantities of overly wet manures. Dry bulking materials can be helpful in offsetting excess pile moisture. However, if the bulking material decomposes too quickly, it can cause the pile or windrow to lose structural integrity and porosity, resulting in poor pile aeration. Examples of commonly used bulking materials already available on the farm include:

- chipped wood,
- sawdust or wood shavings, and
- hay.

The bulk density of the initial mix should not exceed 1,000 pounds per cubic yard to meet the basic aeration and moisture needs of composting microbes. Bulk densities higher than this are a signal that the mix may be too wet or contain materials that are too dense. In either case, compaction and poor aeration will result.

To determine bulk density, follow these steps:

1. Weigh an empty 5-gallon bucket, then fill it with fresh compost mixture and weigh again.
2. Subtract the empty weight from the full bucket weight and record this number.
3. Multiply the number from step 2 by 40.5 to find the bulk density of the compost mix, in pounds per cubic yard. (Rule of thumb: If the weight of compost mix in your 5-gallon bucket exceeds 25 pounds, then your compost mix is probably too dense.)

The Significance of Pile Heating

The heat released from microbial activity inside a compost pile causes a controlled, limited "combustion." Many experienced composters use the term "cooking" to describe the compost process. After successful composting, some of the organic matter from the raw material remains or is changed to humus — the dark brown substance that forms the basis of lasting soil fertility (photo 2-6).

A compost pile's ability to heat and sustain high temperatures is affected by seven factors:

1. physical and biological composition of the composting mass,
2. availability of nutrients, including carbon, to the composting microorganisms,
3. level of moisture in the source ingredients,
4. structure of the pile (particle size, texture, and bulk density),
5. rate of aeration in the pile or windrow,
6. size of the compost pile, and
7. surrounding environment (temperature, wind, humidity, etc.).

Additives

The microbial organisms needed for composting occur naturally in many organic materials. Nevertheless, there are numerous proprietary products being marketed to activate or "jump start" the compost mix. Adding microbial cultures or other activators is sometimes referred to as inoculation or seeding. Although the use of activators may stimulate composting (especially in byproducts that are fairly sterile), most farm composting operations rarely find them necessary. More common types of additives used to control the composting process and improve the quality of the finished product include:

- finished compost that is not too aged and is rich in organisms — for inoculation (up to 10% of compost mass);
- agricultural limestone — to correct calcium deficiencies and moderately low pH values;
- blood or horn meal — to provide nitrogen in the absence of manure;
- bone meal— to correct phosphorus and calcium deficiencies;
- clay soil or pure clay — to enhance formation of clay-humus compounds, especially for use in sandy soils;
- gypsum— to improve soil texture;
- rock phosphate — to add slowly available phosphates;
- sand or coarse granite dust (in small amounts) — to loosen texture and improve drainage;
- seaweed meal — to add potassium and trace elements;
- specific organisms or biodynamic preparations; and
- rock meals or powders — to supply trace mineral elements or clay; also to reduce unpleasant odor, enhance humus formation, and improve drainage.

Odors

If a pile is biologically active, it will be either aerobic (having oxygen), anaerobic (lacking oxygen), or a combination of both. During active composting, aerobic decomposition generates carbon dioxide and water vapor. Active anaerobic decomposition generates carbon dioxide, methane, and other fermentation products that create nuisance odors, lower pile pH, and inhibit plant growth.

Several factors affect odor generation, including oxygen supply, feedstock characteristics, initial pH of the mixture, and additives. Even with a proper oxygen supply (through natural diffusion, turning, or forced aeration), small anaerobic pockets are likely to remain within a pile. However, the byproducts of this anaerobic respiration are degraded when they reach more aerobic environments within the pile. At acidic levels around pH 4.5 or less, aerobic microbes die, equipment corrodes, and odors occur. Low pH and odor are good indicators that more oxygen is needed. For more information on odor management, see "Controlling Odor" on page 46.

pH Adjustment

If very acidic feedstocks (pH < 5.0) such as fruit and vegetable byproducts are being composted, small quantities of wood ash, kiln dust, or other liming products can be added to raise the pH of the initial mix. There are also cases when extremely high pH values may be found in a feedstock (such as when lime is used as bedding in dairy operations), and pH adjustment may be appropriate to help avoid loss of ammonia. Here, as with C:N ratio adjustment, it usually makes sense to improve the imbalance at the front end of the composting process by using a low-cost byproduct as an additive (gypsum or pickling liquor to lower pH, for example).

In most cases, after three days of active composting, the pH of even acidic feedstock begins to rise to approximately 8 or 8.5 and remains there for the balance of the aerobic process. During the subsequent cooling stage, pH usually (but not always) falls slightly until it reaches a value in the range of 7.0–8.0 for mature compost.

Working with Laboratory Reports

As part of recipe making, you may need to determine the percentage of carbon in a feedstock or convert a reported nutrient concentration from a wet ("as is") basis to a dry basis. The following section presents several formulas for converting commonly reported laboratory units into more usable forms.

1. Estimating percent carbon — The carbon content of a feedstock material is sometimes difficult to obtain. If the percentage of nitrogen is known but not the percentage of carbon, then the carbon content can be derived from the C:N ratio (see sidebar on page 38).

   If the laboratory test results or literature report the percentage of volatile solids, then the carbon content can be estimated using the following equation:

   - % carbon = % volatile solids x 0.56

   If laboratory test results or literature report the percentage of ash, then the carbon content can be estimated using the following equation:

   - % carbon = (100 – % ash) x 0.56

2. Converting to a dry basis from a wet or "as is" basis (and vice versa) — Laboratory analyses of nutrient concentrations are usually given on a dry-weight basis (for better comparison between samples with widely different moisture contents). When a report is given on a dry basis, it means the weight percentage of the sample has been reported relative to the weight of the dry solids only. Dry solids are obtained in the laboratory by heating a sample until most of the moisture is driven off. The compost recipe formulas given in this book are based on dry-weight nutrient concentrations.

Sometimes, however, a nutrient concentration is desired on an "as is" or wet basis, since this is the basis on which nutrients are land applied. In order to convert a dry basis nutrient concentration to a wet or "as is" basis, use either of the formulas below.

- % nutrient, wet basis = % nutrient, dry basis x % total solids ÷ 100
- % nutrient, wet basis = % nutrient, dry basis x (100 – % moisture) ÷ 100

EXAMPLE: Converting from a Dry-Weight Basis to a Wet ("As Is") Basis

A wet, semi-solid dairy manure has a reported nitrogen (N) concentration of 3%, dry-weight basis. The lab report also states that the moisture content is 80%. To find the N content of this manure on a wet or "as is" basis, use the second formula listed above:

1. %N, wet basis = 3%N, dry basis x (100 – 80) ÷ 100
2. %N, wet basis = 3%N, dry basis x 0.20
3. %N, wet basis = 0.6%N, wet basis

Recipe Making

The formulation of raw materials in the proper proportions for composting is called recipe making. Five basic principles of successful recipe making are:

1. Know the general conditions needed for composting (table 1-2, page 8).
2. Identify the primary ingredient that must be managed (e.g., poultry litter, separated dairy manure, poultry mortalities, etc.).
3. Know the characteristics of your primary ingredient, including approximate nutrient and carbon contents (or C:N ratio), moisture content, bulk density, pH, and potential for odors.
4. Identify complementary or secondary ingredients that will provide favorable conditions for composting when mixed with the primary ingredient.
5. Create a recipe "blend" that encourages natural, aerobic, high-temperature composting.

NOTE: Compost recipes should be adjusted for special conditions. For example, static piles with no turning will require a mixture with lower initial bulk density; recipes formulated for hot, dry summer composting may require a higher initial moisture content.

Once the ingredients for composting have been identified and the general conditions for composting are understood, the following steps can be used to formulate a compost recipe.

Balancing Moisture

The moisture content within a pile should be maintained between about 40% and 60%. At moisture levels above 60%, water occupies pore space needed for airflow through the pile. Too much water also makes the pile heavy, increasing settling and compaction. Too little moisture causes composting microbes to dry out and cease activity. A quick way to formulate an initial compost mix based on moisture only is outlined below.

1. Determine the moisture content of your primary and secondary ingredients (e.g., chicken manure and sawdust, respectively). See sidebar, page 36, on calculating moisture content.

2. Determine the proper proportions of the two ingredients, on a weight basis, to obtain a mixture with a moisture content around 60%. Table 2-3 presents the weight ratios required to obtain a mixture with 60% moisture using a wide range of moisture contents. [**NOTE:** Table 2-3 is used only to balance moisture. Nevertheless, it can be used as a first approximation when mixing two ingredients of known moisture content. The initial recipe from table 2-3 should be verified and adjusted, as necessary, using standard formulas for compost recipes (see sidebar, page 38).]

The squeeze moisture test is a good way to quickly determine the moisture level of a recipe. A handful of material should feel damp, not dripping wet. If you pick up a handful of material and it drips without being squeezed, it is too wet. For sampling, grab from the interior of the pile in an area that is well mixed, not just the outer shell. If the material appears dry and crumbles after squeezing, it is too dry. If the material retains its clumped shape after squeezing without releasing excess water and your hand is damp, then it is just right for composting (approximately 40–60% moisture). With experience, the squeeze moisture test can be a reliable moisture management tool.

Decomposition of a compost feedstock will slow dramatically if the moisture content falls below 40–45%. Water or other liquid must sometimes be added to dry piles to prevent incomplete composting (see "Controlling Moisture," page 44). If a pile becomes too wet, drier materials such as straw, coarse sawdust, shredded newsprint, or corrugated cardboard can be added. These types of high-carbon materials also work well to balance nitrogen-rich feedstocks such as manures.

TABLE 2-3. Preliminary recipe making for two ingredients using only moisture content

PRIMARY MOISTURE CONTENT

SECONDARY MOISTURE CONTENT	10	20	30	40	50	60	70	80	90	100
10							5:1	2.5:1	1.7:1	1.3:1
20							4:1	2:1	1.3:1	1:1
30							3:1	1.5:1	1:1	1:1.3
40							2:1	1:1	1:1.5	1:2
50							1:1	1:2	1:3	1:4
60						1:1				
70	1:5	1:4	1:3	1:2	1:1					
80	1:2.5	1:2	1:1.5	1:1	2:1					
90	1:1.7	1:1.3	1:1	1.5:1	3:1					
100	1:1.3	1:1	1.3:1	2:1	4:1					

▇ Moisture content too low (< 60%)   ▇ Moisture content too high (> 60%)

Note: Table assumes a desired moisture content of 60%. Table is used only to balance moisture. Nevertheless, it can be used as a first approximation when mixing two ingredients of known moisture content. The initial recipe from this table should be verified and adjusted, as necessary, using standard formulas for compost recipes (see sidebar, page 38).

Problem: Using chicken manure (70% moisture content) as the primary ingredient and sawdust (35% moisture content) as the secondary ingredient, determine the initial recipe proportions for each material to achieve a mixture with a moisture content of approximately 60%.

Solution:

1. Enter table 2-3 under the 70% column for the primary moisture content.

2. For the secondary ingredient (35%), you will have to enter both the 30% and 40% rows (following them all the way to the 70% column).

3. Record the resulting weight ratios for each — 3:1 and 2:1, respectively.

4. Use the average of the two results to find the proper recipe mix, on a weight basis — 2.5:1.

5. Therefore, use 2.5 pounds of chicken manure per 1 pound of sawdust as an initial approximation.

6. Verify and adjust this recipe as necessary by checking the C:N ratio (see sample calculation, "Balancing Materials to the Desired Moisture Content," page 40).

CALCULATING MOISTURE CONTENT, WET BASIS

Calculate the percent moisture for each of the materials you plan to compost.

1. Weigh a small container.

2. Weigh at least 10 grams of the material into the container. Maximize the exposed surface area by using a dish.

3. Dry the sample for 24 hours at 219°F (104°C).

4. Reweigh the sample, subtract the weight of the container, and determine the moisture content using the following equation:

$$M_n = [(W_w - W_d) \div W_w] \times 100$$

where:

M_n = moisture content (%) of material, n, on a wet basis

W_w = wet weight of the sample

W_d = weight of the sample after drying

Suppose, for example, that you weigh 10 grams of a solid manure (W_w) into a 4-gram container and that after drying, the container and manure weigh 6.3 grams. Subtracting out the 4-gram container weight leaves 2.3 grams as the dry weight (W_d) of the manure. Percent moisture would be:

$$M_n = [(W_w - W_d) \div W_w] \times 100$$
$$= [(10 - 2.3) \div 10] \times 100$$
$$= 77\% \text{ moisture content for the manure}$$

NOTE: For in-house testing, it is a good idea to establish a standard sample size that is suited to available containers and equipment. Calculations can sometimes be simplified by using sample sizes that have round numbers, such as 100 grams, 1 pound, or 1 liter. In general, the larger the sample, the more representative the test results.

Balancing Nutrients

The carbon-to-nitrogen (C:N) ratio — which represents the proportion, by weight, of total organic carbon to total nitrogen — is an important requirement for active composting. Raw materials in a compost mix should normally be blended to approximately a 30:1 (weight:weight) C:N ratio.

Carbonaceous material serves mainly as an energy source for composting microbes. Nitrogen is critical for microbial population growth, since it is a major constituent of protein (which forms over 50% of the dry bacterial cell mass). Inadequate nitrogen (high C:N ratio) in a compost mix can result in limited microbial activity and slow feedstock decomposition. Excessive nitrogen (low C:N ratio) can cause losses of gaseous ammonia or water-soluble nitrate, resulting in odors and other environmental problems as well as the loss of valuable plant nutrients. Fortunately, the composting process is forgiving regarding C:N ratios, and a fairly wide C:N range will work well (table 1-2, page 8).

If only two ingredients (e.g., chicken manure plus sawdust) are used for composting, initial recipe proportions by weight can either be assumed or estimated using table 2-3 (page 35). In any case, the resulting C:N ratio of this initial mix should be calculated on a weight basis and checked against desired conditions. Formulas needed to determine the moisture content and C:N ratio of a recipe mix are presented in the sidebar on page 38, including short-cut formulas for mixing only two ingredients. The sample calculation "Balancing Materials to the Desired Moisture Content" (page 40) illustrates this procedure using the chicken manure and sawdust example from page 36.

Developing a recipe based solely on nutrient balance is often done using a "guess and check" strategy, as outlined below.

1. Determine the total carbon, by weight, of the recipe ingredients. (**NOTE:** Carbon availability is variable, depending on the surface area and extent of lignification of the material.)
2. Determine the total nitrogen, by weight, of the ingredients.
3. Divide total carbon by total nitrogen to obtain the C:N ratio of the mixture.
4. Compare to the target C:N ratio.
5. Adjust the weight proportions for feedstock ingredients to bring the C:N ratio and moisture content closer to the optimum. See sample calculation, "Balancing Materials to the Desired C:N Ratio" (page 41).

If three or more ingredients are used, potential recipe formulations can be calculated using the general formulas in the sidebar on page 38 for a mix of materials, or by using more sophisticated numerical methods. If available feedstock ingredients cannot be adjusted to within the desired moisture and C:N ranges, a different set of feedstock materials may need to be considered.

Several computer spreadsheets and programs have been developed to aid in faster recipe preparation. In more advanced computer programs, the user is able to input the target C:N ratio and moisture content. The program then produces a recipe using either user-input or average feedstock data. (The University of Maryland Cooperative Extension has one such recipe-making program.) Another spreadsheet, which uses simultaneous solutions of the C:N and moisture formulas in the sidebar on page 38 for three or four ingredients, is available for downloading at Cornell University's com-

Formulas for Determining Composting Recipes by Weight

Formulas for an Individual Ingredient

$$\text{Moisture content} = \%\text{ moisture content} \div 100$$
$$\text{Weight of water} = \text{total weight} \times \text{moisture content}$$
$$\text{Dry weight} = \text{total weight} - \text{weight of water}$$
$$= \text{total weight} \times (1 - \text{moisture content})$$
$$\text{Nitrogen content} = \text{dry weight} \times (\% N \div 100)$$
$$\% \text{ carbon} = \% N \times C\text{:}N \text{ ratio}$$
$$\text{Carbon content} = \text{dry weight} \times (\% C \div 100)$$
$$= N \text{ content} \times C\text{:}N \text{ ratio}$$

General Formulas for a Mix of Materials

Moisture content =

$$\frac{\text{weight of water in ingredient } a + \text{water in } b + \text{water in } c + \ldots}{\text{total weight of all ingredients}}$$

$$\text{Moisture content} = \frac{(a \times m_a) + (b \times m_b) + (c \times m_c) + \ldots}{a + b + c + \ldots}$$

C:N ratio =

$$\frac{\text{weight of C in ingredient } a + \text{weight of C in } b + \text{weight of C in } c + \ldots}{\text{weight of N in } a + \text{weight of N in } b + \text{weight of N in } c + \ldots}$$

C:N ratio =

$$\frac{[\%C_a \times a \times (1-m_a)] + [\%C_b \times b \times (1-m_b)] + [\%C_c \times c \times (1-m_c)] + \ldots}{[\%N_a \times a \times (1-m_a)] + [\%N_b \times b \times (1-m_b)] + [\%N_c \times c \times (1-m_c)] + \ldots}$$

Symbols:
$$a = \text{total weight of ingredient } a$$
$$b = \text{total weight of ingredient } b$$
$$c = \text{total weight of ingredient } c$$
$$m_a, m_b, m_c, \ldots = \text{moisture content of ingredients } a, b, c, \ldots$$
$$\% N_a, N_b, N_c, \ldots = \% \text{ nitrogen of ingredients } a, b, c, \ldots \text{ (% of dry weight)}$$
$$\% C_a, C_b, C_c, \ldots = \% \text{ carbon of ingredients } a, b, c, \ldots \text{ (% of dry weight)}$$

Shortcut Formulas for Only Two Ingredients
(For example, manure plus straw)

1. Required amount of ingredient a per pound of b based on the desired moisture content:

$$a = \frac{m_b - M}{M - m_a}$$

Then check the C:N ratio using the general formula.

2. Required amount of ingredient a per pound of b based on the desired C:N ratio:

$$a = \frac{\%N_b}{\%N_a} \times \frac{(R - R_b)}{(R_a - R)} \times \frac{(1 - m_b)}{(1 - m_a)}$$

Then check the moisture content using the general formula.

Symbols:
$$a = \text{pounds of ingredient } a \text{ per pound of ingredient } b$$
$$M = \text{desired mix moisture content}$$
$$m_a = \text{moisture content of ingredient } a$$
$$m_b = \text{moisture content of ingredient } b$$
$$R = \text{desired C:N ratio (by weight) of the mix}$$
$$R_a = \text{C:N ratio (by weight) of ingredient } a$$
$$R_b = \text{C:N ratio (by weight) of ingredient } b$$

posting web pages. Information on how to obtain either of these programs can be found in the reference section at the end of this book.

Converting Weight Ratios to Volume Ratios

Unless all feedstock ingredients are weighed prior to mixing (which is not usually the case), the recipe proportions calculated on a weight basis must be converted into volumes of material. Otherwise, bucket operators (who handle materials on a volume basis) will not know how many loads of each ingredient to mix. This weight-to-volume conversion is especially necessary when mixing materials with widely different bulk densities, such as when mixing liquid or semi-solid manures with loose, bulky materials such as straw or hay.

A simplified table for converting weight ratios into volume ratios for material mixing is presented in table 2-4 (page 42). In this table, a bulk density factor is used to convert the weight ratio of each ingredient in a compost recipe into a volume ratio. An illustrative example is presented below.

EXAMPLE: Converting Weight Ratios to Volume Ratios

Problem: What is the volume ratio of a compost recipe that has a calculated weight ratio of 1:3:2, with ingredients corresponding to the following bulk densities?

  Ingredient A (primary) — 900 pounds per cubic yard

  Ingredient B (secondary) — 700 pounds per cubic yard

  Ingredient C (third) — 1,900 pounds per cubic yard

Solution: The first ingredient listed in the weight ratio is always the primary ingredient. Use table 2-4 (page 42) to convert all other ingredients to a volume basis based on the primary ingredient. For conversion, set up the following worksheet:

Ingredient	Bulk density (lbs/cu yd)	Calculated recipe (weight basis)		Relative bulk density factor (from table 2-4)		Recipe ratio (volume basis)
A (primary)	900	1.0	X	1.00	=	1.0
B (secondary)	700	3.0	X	1.29	=	3.87
C (third)	1,900	2.0	X	0.47	=	0.94

Answer: The volume recipe to be used for mixing ingredients A, B, and C is approximately 1:4:1.

Check: To field-verify the accuracy of a calculated recipe as mixed, reverse the above procedure by dividing the actual volume ratio used on-site by the relative bulk density factors from table 2-4 (page 42), as follows:

Ingredient	Bulk density (lbs/cu yd)	Volume ratio, as mixed		Relative bulk density factor (from table 2-4)		Actual recipe, as mixed (weight basis)
A (primary)	900	1	÷	1.00	=	1.00
B (secondary)	700	4	÷	1.29	=	3.10
C (third)	1,900	1	÷	0.47	=	2.13

Sample Calculation: Balancing Materials to the Desired Moisture Content

A farm has chicken manure that usually has a moisture content of 70% when removed from the buildings. Both the moisture and the nitrogen contents are too high for optimum composting, and the manure needs greater porosity. Sawdust is available with a moisture content of 35%. Assume that the C:N ratio of the manure is not more than 10:1 with a nitrogen content of 6% and that the sawdust has a C:N ratio of about 500:1 and a nitrogen content of 0.11%. Determine an appropriate composting recipe.

Using formulas given in the sidebar on page 38:

weight of water = total weight x moisture content
weight of dry matter = total weight − weight of water
weight of nitrogen (N) = weight of dry matter x (%N ÷ 100)
weight of carbon (C) = C:N ratio x weight of N

1 pound of wet manure contains

Water	1 pound x 0.7	=	0.7 pounds
Dry matter	1 pound − 0.7	=	0.3 pounds
N	0.3 x 0.06	=	0.018 pounds
C	0.018 x 10	=	0.18 pounds

1 pound of damp sawdust contains

Water	1 pound x 0.35	=	0.35 pounds
Dry matter	1 pound − 0.35	=	0.65 pounds
N	0.65 x 0.0011	=	0.00072 pounds
C	0.00072 x 500	=	0.36 pounds

The moisture content should not exceed 60%. For 1 pound of wet manure:

$$MC = \frac{\text{weight of water in manure} + \text{weight of water in sawdust}}{\text{total weight}}$$

$$MC = 60\% = 0.6 = \frac{0.7 + (0.35 \times S)}{1 + S}$$

where S is the amount of sawdust needed

$$
\begin{aligned}
MC &= 0.6 (1 + S) = 0.7 + (0.35 \times S) \\
0.25 \, S &= 0.1 \\
S &= 0.4 \text{ pound sawdust per pound of manure} \\
&\quad \text{(or 2.5 pounds manure to 1 pound sawdust)}
\end{aligned}
$$

NOTE: S is calculated from the above equation using a little algebra. Since there are only two ingredients, it is possible to solve for S using the shortcut formulas in the sidebar, "Formulas for Determining Composting Recipes by Weight" (page 38). In this case, S would be the same as b in the sidebar (page 38). The manure would be represented by a. Therefore:

$$S = a = \frac{m_b - M}{M - m_a} = \frac{0.35 - 0.60}{0.60 - 0.70} = \frac{-0.25}{-0.10}$$

S = 2.5 pounds of manure per 1 pound of sawdust

Check the C:N ratio:

$$C:N = \frac{C_{\text{manure}} + C_{\text{sawdust}}}{N_{\text{manure}} + N_{\text{sawdust}}} = \frac{0.18 + (0.4 \times 0.36)}{0.018 + (0.4 \times 0.00072)} = 17.7$$

Since this ratio is near the low end of the acceptable range and the moisture content is at the high end (60%), the amount of sawdust should be increased to raise the C:N ratio.

SAMPLE CALCULATION: BLENDING MATERIALS TO THE DESIRED C:N RATIO

A farm has chicken manure that usually has a moisture content of 70% when removed from the buildings. Both the moisture and the nitrogen contents are too high for optimum composting, and the manure needs greater porosity. Assume that the C:N ratio of the manure is not more than 10:1 with a nitrogen content of 6%. Wheat straw is available that has a moisture content of 15%, a C:N ratio of 128:1, and a nitrogen content of 0.3%. Estimate the amount of straw, S, needed with the chicken manure to obtain a mix C:N ratio of 30. Determine an appropriate composting recipe.

Using formulas given in the sidebar on page 38:

weight of water = total weight x moisture content
weight of dry matter = total weight − weight of water
weight of nitrogen (N) = weight of dry matter x (%N ÷ 100)
weight of carbon (C) = C:N ratio x weight of N

1 pound of wet manure contains

Water	1 pound x 0.7	= 0.7 pounds
Dry matter	1 pound − 0.7	= 0.3 pounds
N	0.3 x 0.06	= 0.018 pounds
C	0.018 x 10	= 0.18 pounds

1 pound of wheat straw contains

Water	1 pound x 0.15	= 0.15 pounds
Dry matter	1 pound − 0.15	= 0.85 pounds
N	0.85 x 0.003	= 0.0026 pounds
C	0.0026 x 128	= 0.33 pounds

The desired C:N ratio is 30:1. For 1 pound of wet manure:

$$C:N = 30 = \frac{(C \text{ in 1 pound manure}) + S \times (C \text{ in 1 pound straw})}{(N \text{ in 1 pound manure}) + S \times (N \text{ in 1 pound straw})}$$

where S is the amount of straw needed

$$30 = \frac{0.18 + S \times (0.33)}{0.018 + S \times (0.0026)}$$

S = 1.4 pounds of straw per pound of manure

NOTE: Again, since only two ingredients are involved, the shortcut formulas in the sidebar on page 38 can be used to solve for S.

$$S = a = \frac{\%N_b}{\%N_a} \times \frac{(R - R_b)}{(R_a - R)} \times \frac{(1 - m_b)}{(1 - m_a)} = \frac{6\%}{0.3\%} \times \frac{(30 - 10)}{(128 - 30)} \times \frac{(1 - 0.70)}{(1 - 0.15)}$$

S = 1.4 pounds of straw per pound of manure

Check the mix moisture content:

$$MC = \frac{\text{weight of water in 1 pound manure} + \text{weight of water in 1.4 pounds straw}}{\text{total weight}}$$

$$MC = \frac{0.7 + (1.4 \times 0.15)}{2.4} = 0.379 = 37.9\%$$

This moisture content is too low for a starting mix. Options include: (1) add water to the mix directly, (2) decrease the amount of straw and accept a lower C:N ratio, (3) add another damp material to the mix, or (4) replace the straw with a wetter amendment.

TABLE 2–4. Bulk density factors used to convert weight ratios into volume ratios

Second or third ingredient bulk density (lbs/cu yd)	Primary ingredient bulk density (lbs/cu yd)									
	100	300	500	700	900	1,100	1,300	1,500	1,700	1,900
100	1.00	3.00	5.00	7.00	9.00	11.00	13.00	15.00	17.00	19.00
300	0.33	1.00	1.67	2.33	3.00	3.67	4.33	5.00	5.67	6.33
500	0.20	0.60	1.00	1.40	1.80	2.20	2.60	3.00	3.40	3.80
700	0.14	0.43	0.71	1.00	1.29	1.57	1.86	2.14	2.43	2.71
900	0.11	0.33	0.56	0.78	1.00	1.22	1.44	1.67	1.89	2.11
1,100	0.09	0.27	0.45	0.64	0.82	1.00	1.18	1.36	1.55	1.73
1,300	0.08	0.23	0.38	0.54	0.69	0.85	1.00	1.15	1.31	1.46
1,500	0.07	0.20	0.33	0.47	0.60	0.73	0.87	1.00	1.13	1.27
1,700	0.06	0.18	0.29	0.41	0.53	0.65	0.76	0.88	1.00	1.12
1,900	0.05	0.16	0.26	0.37	0.47	0.58	0.68	0.79	0.89	1.00

Source: Bill Seekins, Maine Department of Agriculture, Food, and Rural Resources.

DIRECTIONS FOR USING TABLE 2–4:

1. Write down the weight ratio of the final recipe using table 2-3 (page 35) and the sidebar on page 38 ("Formulas for Determining Composting Recipes by Weight") or a computer spreadsheet program. (The first ingredient listed in the weight ratio is always the primary ingredient.)

2. Using table 2-4, determine the bulk density factor of each ingredient with respect to the primary ingredient.

3. Multiply each fraction of the weight ratio by its respective bulk density factor.

4. Use the resulting volume ratio for actual ingredient mixing (e.g., by units or by bucket loads).

5. Table values can also be used the other way to check a formula and recipe. This is done by dividing each fraction of the field recipe mix (volume:volume) by the appropriate bulk density factor to obtain the original (weight:weight) recipe.

Note: See page 39 for an example of how to use this table.

TABLE 2-5. Typical characteristics of selected raw materials

Material	Type of value	%N (dry weight)	C:N ratio (weight: weight)	Moisture content % (wet weight)	Bulk density (lbs/cu yd)
MANURES					
Broiler litter	range	1.6–3.9	13–30	22–46	756–1,026
Cattle:	range	1.5–4.2	11–30	67–87	1,323–1,674
Dairy tie stall	typical	2.7	18	79	–
Dairy freestall	typical	3.7	13	83	–
Horse–general	range	1.4–2.3	22–50	59–79	1,215–1,620
Horse–race track	range	0.8–1.7	29–56	52–67	–
Laying hens	range	4–10	3–10	62–75	1,377–1,620
Sheep	range	1.3–3.9	13–20	60–75	≤1,730
Swine	range	1.9–4.3	5–19	65–91	≤1,620
Turkey litter	average	2.6	16[a]	26	783
STRAW, HAY, SILAGE					
Corn silage	typical	1.2–1.4	38–43[a]	65–68	–
Hay–general	range	0.7–3.6	15–32	8–10	–
Hay–legume	range	1.8–3.6	15–19	–	–
Hay–nonlegume	range	0.7–2.5	–	–	–
Straw–general	range	0.3–1.1	48–150	4–27	58–378
Straw–oat	range	0.6–1.1	48–98	–	–
Straw–wheat	range	0.3–0.5	100–150	–	–
WOOD AND PAPER					
Bark–hardwood	range	0.10–0.41	116–436	–	–
Bark–softwood	range	0.04–0.39	131–1,285	–	–
Corrugated cardboard	typical	0.10	563	8	259
Lumbermill waste	typical	0.13	170	–	–
Newsprint	typical	0.06–0.14	398–852	3–8	195–242
Paper fiber sludge	typical	–	250	66	1,140
Paper mill sludge	typical	0.56	54	81	–
Paper pulp	typical	0.59	90	82	1,403
Sawdust	range	0.06–0.8	100–750	19–65	350–450
Telephone books	typical	0.7	772	6	250
Wood chips	range	–	40–100	–	445–620
Wood–hardwood (chips, shavings, and so on)	range	0.06–0.11	451–819	–	–
Wood–softwood (chips, shavings, and so on)	range	0.04–0.23	212–1,313	–	–

Note: Data were compiled from many references. Where several values are available, the range and average of the values found in the literature are listed. *These should not be considered as the true ranges or averages, just representative values.*

[a] Estimated from ash or volatile solids data.

CHAPTER 3: Process Control and Evaluation

This chapter reviews the basic requirements needed to manage active compost. The section on process control emphasizes the necessary biological conditions. The section on process evaluation includes segments on pile sampling, laboratory testing, process monitoring, recordkeeping, and troubleshooting. At the end of the chapter is a handy troubleshooting guide.

Process Control

Managing Biological Activity

Management of compost biology involves maintaining a suitable environment for microorganisms until decomposition slows to a point where the compost is stable enough to be used. To achieve the desired level of compost stability, the composting process is managed using the following biological parameters:

- nutrients (in proper balance for metabolism),
- oxygen (for respiration),
- moisture (for microbial mobility and enzyme production and secretion),
- temperature (for a hospitable environment), and
- time (sufficient to reach the desired level of decomposition).

Controlling Porosity

During the composting process, pile porosity decreases naturally as the materials decompose and settle under their own weight. Although periodic agitation or turning of piles rebuilds some of this lost porosity, it is best to start with a well-structured mix of materials that resists settling.

If excessive pulverization of materials occurs during pile turning, steps should be taken to:

1. increase the particle size of the initial ingredients,
2. increase the initial proportion of bulking material in the mix,
3. add bulking agent later in the process,
4. increase the particle size of the bulking material,
5. modify the turning equipment (i.e., turner tine configuration, surface speed of tines, and rate of advance through the pile or windrow), or
6. modify the turning schedule to reduce pulverization.

Controlling Moisture

Since much of the decomposition in a compost pile occurs on the liquid surface of individual particles, moisture is essential. If a mixture contains too much water, the water will displace the oxygen supply of respiring microorganisms, causing anaerobic (septic) conditions within the pile and thus a wide range of unpleasant odors. Pile moisture content should be in the 40–60% range (table 1-2, page 8). The squeeze moisture and bulk density tests (pages 35 and 31, respectively) are useful field measurements for process control.

Heat and airflow generated during active composting can evaporate large amounts of water from a pile. Understanding the mechanisms of water loss in a pile is important, because additional water may be needed to prevent premature drying and incomplete stabilization. If a pile gets too dry, it will become biologically dormant, sometimes misleading operators to believe that the compost is finished. In drier climates, compost piles can be given a concave shape (figure 3-1) to trap rainfall within the pile. Moisture can also be added directly to the pile (see sidebar below). When proper moisture is restored to a dry pile, it may take as long as six or seven days for microbes to recolonize and resume activity.

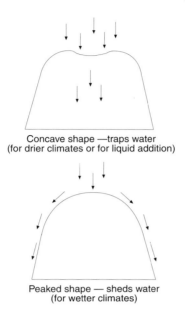

Concave shape —traps water
(for drier climates or for liquid addition)

Peaked shape — sheds water
(for wetter climates)

*If you have persistent problems with
odor, you should check pile oxygen.

FIGURE 3-1. Pile and windrow shapes for moisture control

ADDING LIQUIDS TO A COMPOST PILE

Adding water or other liquids to a compost pile or windrow is sometimes necessary to adjust moisture content or reduce dust. If the volume of water required is small, it can be added during initial feedstock mixing using bucket loaders, batch mixers, pug mills, or rotating drums. Water can also be transported and sprayed from side-delivery tank trucks or wagons, irrigation-style piping systems, or specialized windrow delivery equipment (photo 3-1). Sometimes water is sprayed from a wagon that is followed by a windrow turner. To prevent liquid from simply running down the sides of an existing windrow or pile, it is often necessary to first create a large concave trough at the ridge of the windrow or pile (see figure 3-1) and then apply water into the depression and remix the pile.

Liquid feedstocks such as manure slurries, seafood and vegetable processing liquids, and other nutrient-rich liquids may also be used in composting piles for their moisture, nitrogen, and/or carbohydrate (sugar) content. Some of these liquids present potential odor problems. Consequently, in turned windrow systems, it is usually advisable to contain the liquid material within the windrow prior to turning. This incorporation step can be done using front-end loaders or by injecting liquid materials into the windrow with an agricultural chisel plow, injection hose, and trailing disc (to cover up the furrow). In most cases, windrows are turned only after the liquid is absorbed (usually within one week).

If a turned windrow or pile becomes too moist, a practical way to dry it is to increase the turning frequency. The clouds of moisture evident during turning indicate the release of significant amounts of water (photo 3-2). The increased porosity that results from turning increases diffusion and convective losses of moisture between turnings. Using pile turning as a drying method can be helpful during mild or warm weather. In cold weather, turning removes only a small amount of water, and excessive turning can actually cool the pile. In systems using forced aeration, drying can be accomplished by increasing the airflow rate. In wetter climates, a peaked windrow shape can act like a thatched roof or haystack to help shed rainfall (figure 3-1, page 45). Fabric covers also help.

Controlling Odor

A compost pile is predominantly aerobic if it has a uniform pile oxygen concentration above 5–6%. As oxygen levels decrease below 3%, odors begin to form within the pile due to lack of oxygen for aerobic respiration. If odor problems are persistent, check pile oxygen. Pile oxygen levels can be monitored using a portable analyzer (see "Troubleshooting," page 52).

A 5% oxygen concentration is generally considered the minimum for sustained aerobic composting (table 1-2, page 8). When airflow in a pile is cut off for as short as only two minutes during high microbial activity, the pile can begin to turn anaerobic. Under anaerobic conditions, odors generated by alcohols and volatile organic acids form quickly, lowering pile pH. Reestablishing aerobic conditions through proper aeration and porosity can take from two to six days.

In forced aeration systems such as aerated static piles and in-vessel systems, airflow can be controlled by monitoring pile oxygen, pile temperature, or both. Automated processing systems may employ timer-controlled blowers to maintain oxygen levels above 5%. More highly instrumented composting systems may have monitored temperature sensors to control blowers.

Controlling Temperature

During the initial stages of composting, interior pile temperatures increase rapidly due to active microbial respiration. Higher temperatures are further sustained by self-insulation of the pile, which is directly related to pile size. To avoid overheating, which may immobilize many of the beneficial microorganisms needed for decomposition, many composters turn piles and windrows at a predetermined temperature peak. Many composters try to manage their piles within a general temperature range of 110–150°F (table 1-2, page 8). Pile temperatures can be checked periodically with a dial thermometer or electronic temperature probe (see "Monitoring and Recordkeeping," page 49).

After ten to fifteen days of active composting, most piles, windrows, and vessels reach a temperature level that may be sustained for quite a while, perhaps several months. Thereafter, decomposition rates and pile temperatures gradually decrease, marking the end of active composting and the beginning of the curing stage (see "Compost Curing," page 15).

Pile temperatures in the range shown in table 1-2 (page 8) help maintain a wide variety of microorganisms, including beneficial actinomycetes, bacteria, fungi, algae, and protozoa. A variety of macroorganisms (those visible to the naked eye) can also be found in compost piles, but primarily in the later stages of composting, after heat has subsided. The presence of visible macrofauna such as earthworms, springtails, and mites (figure 3-2) is generally considered to be favorable, suggesting that the compost is near maturity.

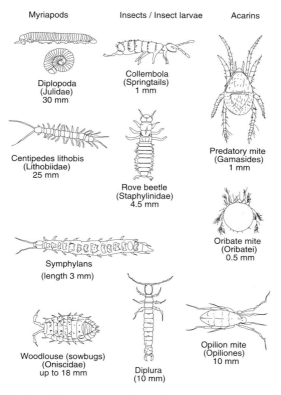

FIGURE 3-2. Beneficial macrofauna observed in composts
Source: Brinton, 1995.

Managing Pathogens

Temperature has an important effect not only on microbial diversity but also on pathogen control. Pathogens are organisms such as bacteria, viruses, fungi, and protozoa that are capable of producing an infection or disease in a susceptible host. If not destroyed or inactivated, pathogenic organisms can be a potential public health concern. Studies have shown that many pathogens are destroyed through composting if all parts of a compost pile are actively managed for temperature and aeration.

Controlling Process Time and Temperature

At least several days of pile temperatures above 130°F are recommended to destroy pathogens and weed seeds. However, pathogen destruction is not solely a high-temperature process. Rather, it is a combination of factors, including natural competition, predation by living organisms, and antibiotic effects within the pile. If a pile is properly mixed and given enough time to attain thorough heating, the temperatures and decompositional changes achieved during active composting are normally sufficient to destroy most on-farm pathogens and weed seeds.

Controlling Pathogen Regrowth

Composting is not a sterilization process. Therefore, regrowth of certain pathogens after active composting is a possibility. Pathogenic bacteria reduced to low levels during active composting may, under some conditions, regrow to higher densities. Viruses and parasites, once reduced in a compost, cannot regrow unless they are reintroduced. Reintroduction of pathogens into stabilized compost can generally be limited by:

- preventing animal access to the compost curing area (recontamination can occur via animals and airborne sources such as bird droppings and weed seeds);
- handling compost with uncontaminated equipment; and
- using only fresh water for make-up after temperatures drop below 130°F.

Regrowth of bacteria appears to be affected by the degree of compost stability. Older composted materials, in general, have lower levels of pathogenic organisms. One possible explanation for this phenomenon is that as the compounds that support bacterial activity are broken down into a more stable compost, bacterial regrowth cannot occur. Consequently, the most effective way to control pathogen regrowth is by ensuring an adequately stabilized compost through attentive process control and careful use of incoming feedstocks.

Process Evaluation

Evaluation of the composting process involves several specific management activities, including:

- sampling and laboratory testing (see below),
- monitoring and recordkeeping (see page 49), and
- troubleshooting (see page 52).

Sampling and Laboratory Testing

To accurately test a feedstock or compost, first obtain a representative sample that reflects the overall quality of the material being tested. As much as possible, samples should be collected immediately before laboratory testing so they do not lose moisture or undergo other changes. If samples cannot be analyzed immediately, they should be placed in an airtight container and refrigerated.

The recommended procedure for sampling a compost pile or feedstock for laboratory analysis is:

1. Use a clean, sterilized 5-gallon bucket and shovel.
2. Take seven samples from all parts of the pile (digging at least 15 inches into the pile for each sample).
3. Mix all seven samples in the bucket thoroughly (for at least one minute).
4. Place about 2 pounds (1 kilogram) of the mixed sample in a sealable plastic bag or sample container provided by the testing laboratory.

Laboratory testing of compost materials is used to:

- formulate a compost recipe,
- evaluate progress in an active pile,
- determine when a compost is ready or mature (see sidebar on page 49), and
- identify the qualities of the finished compost.

Further laboratory testing of finished compost can be used to determine quality characteristics such as pH, soluble salt content, nutrient content, water-holding capacity, organic matter content, particle size and texture, trace elements, and pathogens and weed

How Do You Know When a Compost Is Mature?

Compost used as a soil amendment must be mature so it does not deplete existing soil nutrients, especially nitrogen. If a compost is immature, it will decompose when moisture, temperature, oxygen, and nutrient conditions are favorable. If immature compost is stored or piled under anaerobic conditions where moisture and temperature permit renewed biological activity, odorous and possibly phytotoxic (plant-harmful) compounds can be generated.

The laboratory tests listed below can be used to determine compost maturity. For a more complete description of each test method, refer to *Earth, Plant, and Compost: Principles of Composting for Garden and Farm* (Brinton, 1995) listed in the reference section at the end of this book.

- Common laboratory analyses for quality and maturity:
  - Oxygen consumption – should be low in a mature compost
  - CO_2 respiration – should be low in a mature compost
  - Self-heating ability – should be low in a mature compost
  - Redox potential – should have a high oxidation/reduction value
  - $NO_3:NH_3$ ratio – should have a high ratio (>1)
  - Humus test – should have a relatively high proportion of low- to high-weight humus compounds
- Growth test – cress, barley, green bean, or radish seeds should germinate in a compost mixture at the proper time and produce vigorous, healthy plants (photo 3-3).
- Dewar maturity test – measures heating potential of a compost in a special flask that contains the heat loss. Compost in the flask should not rise more than approximately 18°F above ambient temperature after three to five days.
- Nitrate and ammonia tests – nitrate values should be no more than 200 parts per million; no significant ammonia should be detectable in a mature compost.
- Colorimetric respiration procedure – test shows grades of compost respiration in a gel that changes color under exposure to respired carbon dioxide from a sealed compost sample. A pre-specified color denotes a mature "finished" compost.

seeds. Figure 3-3 on page 50 shows a sample laboratory report. Most compost users consider a good compost to have the following general characteristics:

1. a homogeneous appearance that is dark brown or black in color,
2. an earthy smell with no objectionable odor,
3. a particle size of less than one-half inch,
4. stability (capability of being stored for a reasonable time without losing its effectiveness as a soil amendment),
5. no weed seeds,
6. no phytotoxins or visible contaminants, and
7. a pH of 6.0–7.8.

Monitoring and Recordkeeping

Keeping records of all feedstock materials used in the composting operation is strongly recommended. Records can include the type, amount, source, date available, and condition of feedstock ingredients. Feedstock quantities are commonly measured and reported using volume and weight. The use of volume as a measure of quantity can be misleading, however. For example, 1 cubic yard of loose,

Account: 641
SAMPLE REPORT
Client Farm
Rural Route
Waterville ME 04901

Date Received: 9-19-90
Date Reported: 10-2-90
Lab ID Number: 1907.2

Sample Identification: Fresh Cow Manure 1990

VARIABLE MEASURED	Unit	dry basis	as is basis	pounds/ton *as is*
DENSITY	lbs·ft³	9	53	1,440 lbs/yd³
Solids	%	100.0	17.1	342
Moisture	%	0.0	82.9	199 gals
Est. Water Holding Capacity	%	257.5	72.0	173 gals
pH (1:1 H₂0)	-logH⁺	▭	8.23	-
Organic Matter	%	84.6	14.5	289
Conductivity	mmhos·cm⁻¹	▭	3.8	-
Carbon: Nitrogen (C:N) Ratio	w:w	29.3	29.3	-
Oxidation/Reduction (ORP) Value		378/114	(low)	-
...................Mineral Nutrients...................				
Total Nitrogen	%	1.671	0.286	5.7
Organic-N	%	1.271	0.217	4.3
Ammonium-N (NH₄-N)	ppm	4004	685	1.4
Volatile N as % of Total-N	w:w	▭	2.3	-
Phosphorus (P)	%	0.952	0.163	3.3
Potassium (K)	%	0.870	0.149	3.0
Sodium (Na)	%	0.587	0.100	2.0
Calcium (Ca)	%	11.506	1.968	39.4
Magnesium (Mg)	%	0.886	0.152	3.0

Notes: ppm (mg/kg) = percentage x 10,000
< = less than MLD (minimum level of detection) for the particular mineral tested
FORM 101.b Copyright © WOODS END RESEARCH LABORATORY, Inc.

FIGURE 3-3. Sample laboratory report
Adapted with permission from Woods End Research Laboratory, Inc.

unbundled hay is a very different quantity than 1 cubic yard of highly compacted manure. More importantly, the bulk density of a material changes. As much as possible, ingredients should be expressed in terms of weight, and their weight recorded upon collection or delivery.

Recipe formulations should also be recorded, including the date they were mixed and any assigned pile numbers. In larger operations, a sketch showing the location of each numbered pile (including curing piles) may be helpful. A well-maintained recordkeeping system can help the operator plan for normal seasonal fluctuations in raw materials.

Compost process temperatures should be monitored and recorded frequently, even after the composter becomes familiar with the process. A dial thermometer with a 3- to 5-foot stem is recommended for low-cost monitoring of pile temperatures. The thermometer should have a temperature range of approximately 0–200°F. Thermometers should be equipped with a calibration screw and should be calibrated regularly by submersion in ice water (32°F). A pointed tip helps the thermometer pass through clumps of material and lowers the risk of breaking the stem. If a dial thermometer does not readily pass into the compost pile or windrow, bulk density may be higher than recommended, resulting in poor pile aeration. In this case, additional (or less stiff) bulking agent may be required. Figure 3-4 shows a dial thermometer and a probe with digital readout for manual monitoring of compost pile temperatures. Electronic thermometers are recommended where temperatures are taken often in many places.

Temperature testing is recommended at 1- and 3-foot depths along both sides of the windrow at 20-foot intervals. Temperatures should be checked in the same location in the pile each day. Since daily

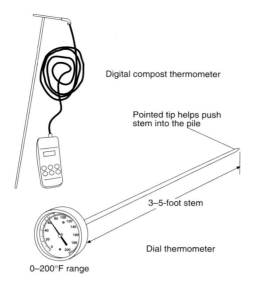

Digital compost thermometer

Pointed tip helps push stem into the pile

3–5-foot stem

Dial thermometer

0–200°F range

FIGURE 3-4. Instruments for measuring windrow/pile temperatures

temperature monitoring may not be cost-effective on small farms (particularly at 20-foot intervals), daily temperatures may be monitored at 100-foot intervals. Figure 3-5 presents a sample form used for monitoring and recording pile information.

The University of Maine Compost School recommends that piles or windrows should be turned: (1) at approximately 150°F, (2) if the temperature drops without cause, or (3) if the difference between 1-foot and 3-foot temperature readings is greater than 20°F.

Pile Monitoring Record

Date _____ Time of day _____

Data collected by_____

Weather (sunny, raining, and so on)_____

Ambient (air) temperature_____ °F   Wind direction _____

General site observations and comments_____

_____

_____

_____

Pile number	Moisture rating	Odor rating	Temperature (°F)		Distance from end of pile	Comments
			1-Foot depth	3-Foot depth	Feet	

Recorded By Date

FIGURE 3-5. Sample form for monitoring and recording pile information

With the use of computer software and graphics packages, daily and weekly temperature profiles can be produced for a better picture of pile performance (see figure in sidebar, page 17). Daily and weekly trends in temperature suggest how often turning is required. A normal pattern should emerge after several batches have been successfully composted. Deviations from the normal temperature pattern indicate that changes have occurred that might need correction (such as poor initial mixing of feedstock ingredients). Although temperature is important, it is only one of several indicators used to manage an active pile or windrow (see "Troubleshooting" below).

Troubleshooting

Five basic conditions are needed for active composting:

1. free moisture — to act as a bacterial medium and nutrient solution,

2. oxygen/airspace (porosity) — to supply air to aerobic and facultative anaerobes,

3. energy source — namely carbon or volatile organic solids,

4. nitrogen — for protein synthesis of composting organisms, and

5. pH — near neutral (7.0), for a hospitable microbial environment and to retain ammonia in solution.

Temperature and odor are the most important indicators of how well composting is progressing. Strong putrefying odors from a composting material are a sign that something is wrong — that excessive anaerobic conditions exist. If anaerobic conditions are excessive, a pile or windrow may require turning or a more porous mix of feedstocks. Active, hands-on management of the composting process is an essential element of troubleshooting.

Temperature is the primary measure for monitoring the composting process, because the heat produced during composting is directly related to microbial activity. Abnormally low temperatures signal that aerobic microbial activity has declined. Low temperatures could be caused by low pile moisture or freezing conditions. Low pile moisture can be checked using the squeeze moisture test (see "Balancing Moisture," page 34). Normally, low temperatures signal the need for turning, unless the compost is nearing the end of the active composting process.

If the compost pile temperature does not recover after turning or aeration and the composting process is not nearing normal completion time, you should suspect some other problem (see sidebar on page 53). Low temperatures accompanied by odors point to a lack of oxygen, which can mean the composting materials are too wet or poorly mixed. In piles or windrows that are not evenly mixed, there may be low temperatures in some sections of the pile while other sections are well heated.

Oxygen monitoring equipment is commonly used in conjunction with thermometers to troubleshoot composting piles. Oxygen sensors measure the oxygen level within a pile, providing a clue to the current state of the composting process. Oxygen-sensing instruments can be used to monitor the oxygen concentration in:

- raw feedstock,
- actively composting piles,
- curing piles, and
- stored, finished compost.

A 3–5% oxygen concentration is generally considered the minimum for sustained aerobic composting (table 1-2, page 8). A portable oxygen analyzer with a perforated probe and digital readout is illustrated in figure 3-6. Portable oxygen testing equipment can be purchased for approximately $1,000. The oxygen probe should reach the center of the pile. Oxygen-sensing equipment is generally more expensive and complex than temperature-sensing equipment. Combination probes that measure temperature and oxygen are available. When used together, pile temperature and oxygen levels provide a very good indication of process conditions. Table 3-1 beginning on page 55 presents a detailed guide to troubleshooting a compost pile.

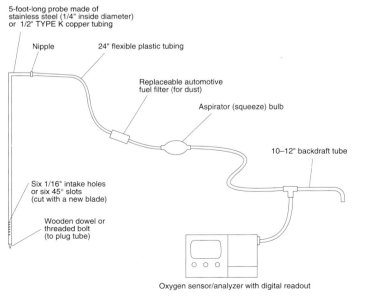

5-foot-long probe made of stainless steel (1/4" inside diameter) or 1/2" TYPE K copper tubing

Nipple

24" flexible plastic tubing

Replaceable automotive fuel filter (for dust)

Aspirator (squeeze) bulb

10–12" backdraft tube

Six 1/16" intake holes or six 45° slots (cut with a new blade)

Wooden dowel or threaded bolt (to plug tube)

Oxygen sensor/analyzer with digital readout

FIGURE 3-6. Oxygen-analyzing equipment

Seasonal and Weather Problems

Seasonal and weather variations in farm composting operations call for operational adjustments that compensate for or take advantage of changing conditions. Many farmers are surprised to learn that outdoor composting can continue year-round, even in cold climates. In many outdoor compost operations, high pile temperatures prevent snow from collecting on top of compost piles. High internal pile temperatures during cold weather are evidenced by water vapor rising from active piles, especially during and after turning (photo 3-2).

Nevertheless, cold weather does slow composting by increasing the heat loss from a windrow or pile. In cases of extreme cold and high pile moisture, the entire windrow may freeze, temporarily halting the composting process. To avoid problems during cold conditions, combine or enlarge windrows and piles so they retain more heat. To generate enough heat to prevent freezing, piles should be at least 5 feet high. Since older, more stable compost generates less heat, older piles should be at least 8 feet high if they are to be composted or cured through the winter.

Warm weather enhances water loss by evaporation from the windrow/pile surface. This can be an advantage if a drier compost is desired; however, water must be added to piles if they become too dry (see sidebar, "Adding Liquids to a Compost Pile," page 45). In regions with excessively hot summers, such as the southwestern United States, water or other liquids may be needed to wet the piles for continued microbial activity.

Unusually wet weather can create problems in outdoor composting facilities. Open puddles or piles of saturated feedstock or compost may lead to odor problems and poor neighbor relations. Although windrows or piles normally absorb rainfall or snow without causing pile saturation, they can become wetter than desired under prolonged wet weather conditions. Special covers for windrows (such as fleece) seem to work well in keeping water out. If the windrow becomes too wet, more turnings will be required to evaporate the added moisture.

The most difficult challenge related to excessive precipitation on natural soil sites is the muddy conditions that make it difficult to operate equipment (photo 3-4). Puddles and standing water can also cause anaerobic conditions at the base of the windrow or pile and lead to insect and odor problems. Good site drainage is crucial. In the winter, snow usually melts from outdoor windrows, but it will still need to be plowed between windrows to allow equipment travel. Snow mixed with compost needs to be stored so that melt water is not discharged directly into clean streams or water bodies.

Seasonal changes can influence the availability of raw materials. Some crop residues and food processing residuals are a good example (photos 2-1 through 2-4). Available primarily in the fall, these materials must be composted in large quantities or stored safely for gradual use with other feedstock materials. Seasonal changes can also affect compost use.

TABLE 3-1. Troubleshooting guide

Condition or situation	Possible source or reason	Other clues	Remedy
Pile fails to heat	Materials too dry	Cannot squeeze water from material	Add water or wet ingredients
	Materials too wet	Materials look or feel soggy; pile slumps; moisture content greater than 60%	Add dry amendments and remix
	Not enough nitrogen, or slowly degrading or stable materials	C:N ratio greater than 50:1; large amount of woody materials	Add high-nitrogen ingredients; change composting recipe
	Poor structure	Pile settles quickly; few large particles; not excessively wet	Add bulking agent
	Cold weather and small pile size	Pile height less than 3.5 feet	Enlarge or combine piles; add highly degradable ingredients
	pH excessively low	pH measures less than 5.5; garbage-like odor	Add lime or wood ash and remix
Temperature falls consistently over several days	Low oxygen; need for aeration	Temperature declines gradually rather than sharply	Turn or aerate pile
	Low moisture	Cannot squeeze water from material	Add water

continued on next page

TABLE 3-1. Troubleshooting guide *(continued)*

Condition or situation	Possible source or reason	Other clues	Remedy
Uneven temperatures or varying odors in pile	Poorly mixed materials	Visible differences in the pile moisture and materials	Turn or remix pile
	Uneven airflow or air short circuiting	Visible differences in the pile moisture and materials	Shorten aeration pipe; remix pile
	Materials at different stages of maturity	Temperature varies along the pile length	None required
Gradually falling temperatures; pile does not reheat after turning or aeration	Composting nearing completion	Approaching expected composting time period; adequate moisture available; C:N ratio less than 20:1	None required
	Low moisture	Cannot squeeze water from materials	Add water and remix
Pile overheating (temperatures greater than 150°F)	Insufficient aeration for heat removal	Pile is moist	Turn pile or increase the airflow rate
	Moderate to low moisture; limited evaporative cooling	Pile feels damp but not excessively dry or wet	Add water; continue turning and aeration to control temperature
	Pile is too large	Height greater than 8 feet	Decrease the pile size

continued on next page

TABLE 3-1. Troubleshooting guide *(continued)*

Condition or situation	Possible source or reason	Other clues	Remedy
Extremely high temperatures (greater than 170°F) in pile: composting or curing/storage	Pyrolysis or spontaneous combustion	Low moisture content; pile interior looks or smells charred	Decrease pile size; maintain proper moisture content; add water to charred or smoldering sections; break down pile, combine with other piles
High temperatures or odors in curing or storage pile	Compost is not stable	Short active composting period; temperature and odor change after mixing	Manage pile for temperature and odor control, turn piles as necessary; limit pile size
	Piles are too large	Height greater than 8 feet; width greater than 20 feet	Decrease pile size
Ammonia odor coming from composting piles	High nitrogen level	C:N ratio less than 20:1	Add high-carbon amendments
	High pH	pH greater than 8.0	Lower pH with acidic ingredients and/or avoid alkaline ingredients
	Slowly available carbon source	Large woody particles; C:N ratio less than 30:1	Use another carbon amendment or increase the carbon proportion

continued on next page

TABLE 3-1. Troubleshooting guide *(continued)*

Condition or situation	Possible source or reason	Other clues	Remedy
Rotten-egg or putrid odors coming from composting piles continually	Anaerobic conditions	Low temperatures	
	• Materials too wet		Add dry amendment
	• Poor structure		Add bulking agent
	• Pile compacted		Remix pile, add bulking agent if necessary
	• Insufficient aeration		Turn pile or increase the airflow rate
	Anaerobic conditions	High temperatures	
	• Pile too large		Decrease the pile size
	• Airflow uneven or short circuiting		Remix pile; change recipe
Odors generated only after turning	Odorous raw materials	High temperatures	Frequent turnings; increase porosity; add odor-absorbing amendment
	Insufficient aeration; anaerobic interior	Falling temperatures	Shorten time interval between turnings; increase porosity

continued on next page

TABLE 3-1. Troubleshooting guide *(continued)*

Condition or situation	Possible source or reason	Other clues	Remedy
Site-related odors (piles not odorous)	Raw materials	Odor is characteristic of the raw materials	Handle raw materials promptly with minimal storage
	Nutrient-rich puddles because of poor drainage	Standing puddles of water; ruts in pad	Divert runoff away; maintain pad surface
	Holding pond or lagoon overloaded with nutrients or sediment	Heavy algae and weed growth; gas bubbles on pond surface	Install sediment trap; enlarge pond surface area; use runoff and pond water on cropland
Fly or mosquito problems	Flies breeding in compost piles	Fresh manure or food material at pile surface; flies hover around piles	Turn piles every four to seven days; cover static piles with a 6-inch layer of compost
	Flies breeding in raw materials	Wet raw materials stored on site more than four days	Handle raw materials promptly
	Mosquitoes breeding in stagnant water	Standing puddles of water; nutrient-rich pond or lagoon	Grade site properly; maintain pad surface; maintain holding pond or lagoon in aerobic condition

continued on next page

TABLE 3-1. Troubleshooting guide *(continued)*

Condition or situation	Possible source or reason	Other clues	Remedy
Compost contains clumps of materials and large particles; texture is not uniform	Poor mixing of materials or insufficient turning	Original raw materials discernible in compost	Screen compost; improve initial mixing
	Airflow uneven or short circuiting	Wet clumps of compost	Screen or shred compost; improve air distribution
	Raw materials contain large particles and nondegradable or slowly degradable materials	Large, often woody, particles in compost	Screen compost; grind and/or sort raw materials
	Active composting not complete	Curing piles heat or develop odors	Lengthen composting time or improve composting conditions

CHAPTER 4: Site Considerations, Environmental Management, and Safety

This chapter is divided into three sections: site considerations, nuisance control, and safety. The chapter begins by presenting some basic site considerations, including buffer zones and area requirements for windrows. In the second section, management practices for controlling environmental and other nuisances are outlined. At the end of the chapter, safety issues such as equipment safety, accident prevention, operator health, spills, and fires are addressed.

Site Considerations

Buffer Zones

Buffer zones between farm composting operations and nearby streams, water sources, and residences are intended to lessen water quality concerns as well as nuisance factors such as odor and equipment noise. For surface water protection, the horizontal separation distance from the compost facility and a surface water body is important. For groundwater protection, the vertical separation distance between the compost pad surface and the seasonal high water table is critical.

Table 4-1 lists suggested vertical and horizontal separation distances for composting facilities. Although separation distances shown in table 4-1 can be somewhat arbitrary, they provide guidance for locating composting sites in sensitive areas. Farmers should consider having an experienced engineer or other qualified professional evaluate the potential for pollution at each proposed site.

TABLE 4-1. Commonly recommended separation distances for composting facilities

Sensitive area	Minimum separation distance (feet)
Property line	50 (ideal 500)
Residence or place of business	200 (ideal 2,000)
Private well or other potable water source	100
Wetlands or surface water (streams, ponds, lakes)	100
Subsurface drainage pipe or drainage ditch discharging to a natural water course	25
Water table (seasonal high)	3
Bedrock	3

Adapted from *On-Farm Composting Handbook* (NRAES–54).
Note: Actual separation distances will depend on regulations and practices in specific jurisdictions as well as site-specific factors. Check with your local or regional water quality authority, health department, or environmental/conservation district. Farmers should consider having an experienced engineer or other qualified professional evaluate the potential for pollution at a proposed composting site.

Area Requirements

For turned (or static) windrows and piles, the surface area required for a composting pad depends on the volume of material handled, the shape of the pile or windrow, and the space needed to maneuver equipment. The cross-sectional shape of the pile is determined by the composting method and the type of equipment used to build and/or turn the windrows. Table 1-3 on page 12 presents approximate volumes, in cubic yards per 100 feet of windrow, for various pile shapes. Figures 1-4 and 1-5 on pages 11 and 12, respectively, provide basic dimensions and formulas needed to estimate the composting pad area for a given volume of material.

The sample calculation on page 63 presents a step-by-step procedure for sizing a compost pad. When estimating area requirements for curing and storage, note that the volume of finished compost is roughly half the volume of the original material. In addition to volume reduction, composting materials also experience a large weight reduction, on the order of 40–80%, because of water and carbon loss (as carbon dioxide, CO_2).

Area requirements for compost curing and storage vary considerably, from 25% to 200% of the size of the composting area. Within limits imposed to prevent anaerobic conditions (and the possibility of fire), the piled height of stored compost is determined mainly by the reach of available loaders. Space requirements for curing and storage of compost depend on:

1. the volume of finished compost,
2. the length of time required for curing and storage,
3. pile height and spacing, and
4. equipment movement.

Nuisance Control

A compost site must be operated in a responsible manner to safeguard public health, safety, and the environment. Minimizing or eliminating nuisances — such as odors, runoff, vectors, dust, traffic, and noise — has public health as well as environmental and aesthetic benefits.

Odor Control

Odor problems present the biggest single threat to a composting operation. Although odors are not harmful at the concentrations found around composting sites, they can be a nuisance to nearby residents. The best defense against odor complaints is effective management. The second best defense is distance between neighbors and the composting site. Where these are not possible, some form of odor control or treatment is necessary.

Four principal causes of odors at a composting operation are:

1. odorous raw materials,
2. poor site conditions,
3. ammonia lost from high-nitrogen materials, and
4. excessive anaerobic conditions within windrows and piles.

The most common cause of odors is wet, highly decomposable feedstocks (such as manures, food processing residuals, fish processing byproducts, etc.) that are delivered to or generated at a site. These types of organic residuals that decompose rapidly are known as putrescible materials. Nuisances such as flies and odors often accompany these materials. Many odors can be avoided at the outset by

- providing extra carbon in the compost mix,
- processing potentially odorous materials promptly,

SAMPLE CALCULATION: DETERMINING THE REQUIRED AREA AND LAYOUT OF THE COMPOSTING PAD

Manure from sixty thousand laying hens is to be composted with green sawdust. The farmer will use the windrow composting method and turn the windrows with a bucket loader. The estimated composting period is sixty days. The compost will be cured for one month (thirty days) and then may be stored for up to three months (ninety days) before being land applied. Assume that the compost volume is 50% of the volume of the raw materials.

Estimated Composting Pad Area

1. Estimate the daily volume of material to be composted:

   a. Manure. From table 2-2 (page 30), one laying hen produces approximately 0.0035 cubic foot (cu ft) of manure per day

   $$60,000 \text{ birds} \times \frac{0.0035 \text{ cu ft manure}/\text{day}}{\text{bird}} = \frac{210 \text{ cu ft manure}}{\text{day}}$$

   b. Sawdust. Assume that the composting recipe calls for 3 volumes of sawdust per volume of manure (equal parts by weight).

   $$\frac{3 \text{ cu ft sawdust}}{\text{cu ft manure}} \times \frac{210 \text{ cu ft manure}}{\text{day}} = \frac{630 \text{ cu ft sawdust}}{\text{day}}$$

   Total daily volume of ingredients = 210 + 630

   $$= 840 \text{ cu ft per day}$$

   Account for a 20% volume reduction in combining the materials (that is, multiply by 0.80).

   Estimated daily volume of mix = 840 x 0.80

   $$= 672$$

   $$= \text{approximately 700 cu ft per day}$$

2. Determine the volume of material on the composting pad:

   Total material volume = 60 days x 700 cu ft per day

   $$= 42,000 \text{ cu ft}$$

   The windrows will be combined as they shrink in volume, freeing space on the pad for new windrows. Assume a shrinkage factor of 0.75.

   Adjusted total material volume = 42,000 cu ft x 0.75

   $$= 31,500 \text{ cu ft}$$

3. Determine windrow dimensions:

   Assume that the site allows 150-foot-long windrows and that the bucket loader can build windrows 8 feet high and 14 feet wide. Assume that these dimensions allow adequate air movement through the windrows.

4. Calculate the estimated windrow volume:

   From figure 1-4 (page 11), the windrow cross-sectional area is:

   A = 2/3 x b x h = 2/3 x 14 x 8 = approximately 75 square feet

   Therefore, the windrow volume, in cubic yards, is:

   Volume = A (sq ft) x length (ft) = 75 sq ft x 150 ft

   $$= 11,250 \text{ cu ft} \div 27 \text{ cu ft/cu yd} = 417 \text{ cu yd}$$

   OR from table 1-3 (page 12): The volume of an 8-foot-high by 14-foot-wide windrow is 277 cubic yards per 100 feet of windrow — or 416 cubic yards for a 150-foot windrow.

— continued on next page —

5. Determine the number of windrows required:

$$\text{\# windrows} = \frac{\text{Total material volume}}{\text{Single windrow volume}} = \frac{31,500 \text{ cu ft}}{11,250 \text{ cu ft}} = 2.8$$

Use 3 windrows.

6. Lay out the windrow spacing, and determine estimated pad width.

NOTE: The windrows will require several turnings before they can be combined, so they must be spaced to allow equipment movement on both sides. From figure 1-5 (page 12):

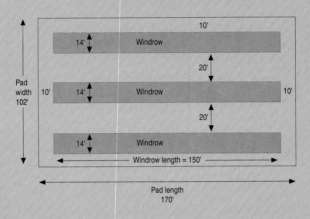

Overall pad dimensions:

102 ft wide x 170 ft long = 17,340 sq ft

Estimated Curing Area

Assume that the curing piles are 6 feet high and 18 feet wide with an average height of 4 feet and that they are stacked toe-to-toe (no space between piles).

1. Estimate the volume of compost in curing area:

700 cu ft per day x 30 days x 0.50 shrinkage factor = 10,500 cu ft

2. Determine the area occupied by the curing piles:

$$\text{Curing area} = \frac{\text{Curing volume}}{\text{Average pile height}} = \frac{10,500 \text{ cu ft}}{4 \text{ ft}}$$

$$= 2,625 = \text{approximately 2,700 sq ft}$$

3. Lay out the area accounting for pile spacing and equipment access (see below).

Estimated Compost Storage Area

Assume that the compost is stored in adjacent piles at an average height of 8 feet.

1. Estimate the volume in the storage area:

700 cu ft per day x 90 days x 0.50 shrinkage = 31,500 cu ft

2. Determine the area occupied by the storage piles:

$$\text{Storage area} = \frac{\text{Storage volume}}{\text{Average pile height}} = \frac{31{,}500 \text{ cu ft}}{8 \text{ ft}}$$

$$= 3{,}938 = \text{approximately 4,000 sq ft}$$

3. Lay out the area accounting for pile spacing and equipment access (see below).

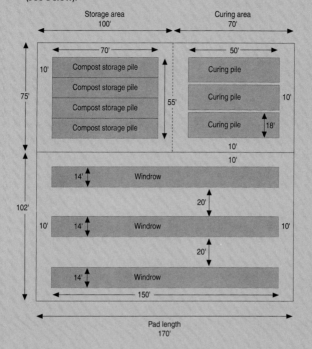

NOTE: This layout shows the minimum area required for the situation given by this example. In an actual operation, additional space might be needed for piles/windrows that are being constructed or removed plus areas for raw material storage, grinding, screening, and so on.

- keeping pH in the neutral range,
- providing proper site drainage, and
- maintaining proper aeration, moisture, and temperature.

Odor Identification

Composting odors are a mix of many different chemical compounds. When identifying odors, avoid quick judgments. Often, a secondary odor is the most obvious odor at the site, while a more pervasive (primary) odor is transported for miles. For example, odors such as ammonia may dissipate quickly, leaving more pervasive organic acids to be detected off-site.

Many odors from a composting process result from the anaerobic fermentation of organic materials, principally carbohydrates and proteins in the feedstock. Carbohydrates contain carbon, hydrogen, and oxygen in compounds such as cellulose and sugars, which readily decompose under anaerobic conditions and produce odorous compounds such as alcohols, esters, aldehydes, phenols, and volatile organic acids (VOAs). Proteins contain carbon, hydrogen, nitrogen, oxygen, and sulfur, which produce odorous compounds such as ammonia, amines, and mercaptans (sulfur-containing compounds).

The five general classes of odorous compounds associated with composting are:

- *Nitrogen* — including ammonia, amines, and indoles. Ammonia is a product of both aerobic and anaerobic decomposition. Most people recognize the smell of ammonia, which is more readily released at a pile pH above 7.5. Amines have a similar odor but also a "fishy" smell. Aerobic decomposition generates ammonia if the C:N ratio is less than about 20:1 (nitrogen-rich). Another nitrogen compound is skatole of the indole group, which is formed when animal or human wastes break down. Skatole is a relatively short-lived compound, but it creates an unpleasant fecal odor.

- *Sulfur* — including hydrogen sulfide, organic sulfides, and mercaptans. Most recognizable is the rotten egg smell of hydrogen sulfide. Organic sulfides such as dimethyl sulfide and dimethyl disulfide produce intense odors ranging from "garlicky" to a "dead animal" odor. Another sulfur-containing odorant is mercaptans. Typical mercaptans are methyl mercaptan and ethyl mercaptan. Utilities inject mercaptans, which can smell like leeks or rotten cabbage, into natural gas (in the parts per billion range) to give natural gas an odor. With manures and food scraps, mercaptans and organic sulfides are an issue. A pile pH greater than 6.0 promotes hydrogen sulfide and mercaptan generation. Aerobic decomposition reduces these sulfides to odorless sulfates.

- *Volatile organic acids* — VOAs, including acetic, propionic, and butyric acids. VOAs occur when fatty acids decompose either aerobically or anaerobically. Under aerobic conditions, the VOAs are oxidized quickly to carbon dioxide and water. Under anaerobic conditions, VOAs do not decompose rapidly. Their smell has been described as similar to "old vomit." The sour smell of bagged grass clippings comes from VOAs. Pile oxygen concentrations below 3% promote VOA accumulation.

- *Terpenes* — Terpenes are formed when wood chips, brush, or sawdust is decomposed through composting. Terpenes can be a problem in curing piles containing wood chips. Wood mulch, when freshly applied, has the biting terpene odor of anaerobic decomposition until the odor is dissipated by aerobic decomposition. Processing of fresh yard trimmings releases terpenes through grinding.

- *Other organics* — including aldehydes, ketones, and alcohols. These compounds form during decomposition of biosolids and food scraps and are not as odorous or prevalent as the other groups above.

Generally, organic sulfides have the highest odor intensities, followed by mercaptans, indoles, amines, organic acids, ammonia, and terpenes. Odors usually contain many compounds, so identifying them is somewhat difficult. The following list is intended as a guide to identifying some of the odors likely to be encountered in a farm composting operation. If it smells like:

- vomit or body odor (BO), it is volatile organic acids;
- emissions from a wood pulping plant, it is organic sulfides and mercaptans;
- natural gas, it is mercaptans;
- something dead or rotting, it is organic sulfides;
- manure or human feces, it is skatole (indoles); and
- turpentine or wood mulch, it is terpenes.

Odor Control via Process Improvements

The best way to prevent odors is through good management (see sidebar below). Maintaining aerobic conditions in a pile is one of the best ways to minimize odors. Keeping the compost site clean is another effective method of odor control. Piles of unused feedstocks should be kept dry; wet, nitrogen-rich materials should be composted as soon as possible to reduce the risk of odorous anaerobic conditions. Anaerobic conditions in stored piles are minimized by preventing on-site standing water. On-site dust can carry odors and should be minimized.

Many odor problems can be solved by immediately mixing nitrogenous raw materials with a balanced source of carbon. Wet, odor-generating organics such as manure slurries or raw food residuals may be placed in a windrow that has been opened up. These materials may be layered with a dry, high-carbon material. If necessary, a cover of finished compost 6–8 inches thick can be used to limit odor releases. The base of these windrows should be constructed of absorbent bulking material to provide aeration and absorb moisture. After the windrow has begun heating, it can be turned. When active windrows are turned, odors may be released briefly. Thereafter, windrows can be turned for temperature control when pile temperatures reach approximately 150°F (see "Monitoring and Recordkeeping," page 49).

Often, the most effective way to correct overly wet or anaerobic conditions in a pile is to blend in dry materials or remix the pile (for drying). This allows odorous anaerobic compounds to decompose or evaporate into odorless carbon dioxide and water.

Any odor-releasing activities (such as windrow turning, pile mixing, movement of odorous materials, etc.) should be scheduled so as to minimize the impact of odors on neighbors. For example, postpone activities that release odors if the wind is blowing toward the most sensitive neighbors. Avoid turning windrows on hot, still summer days or holidays and weekends when people are more likely to be outside.

Small concentrations of nuisance odors can be masked or neutralized with commercially available chemicals. Although these products are available at a modest cost, they act only temporarily. Larger odor concentrations require more expensive treatment systems, such as chemical scrubbers and biofilters. Biofilters may work well but require maintenance.

STEPS TO CONTROL ODOR THROUGH PILE MANAGEMENT

- Establish and maintain pile porosity at 40% or greater.
- Mix appropriate materials to continually eliminate any clumps in the pile.
- Keep pile height low enough to avoid compaction.
- Aerate to keep pile oxygen concentration above 3%.
- Operate on a high C:N ratio (> 30) to prevent excess ammonia release.
- Keep pile moisture content between 45% and 60%.
- Ensure good pile drainage — do not allow ponding beneath, around, or between piles.

In lieu of expensive and impractical biofiltration, many farm composters simply add a 6–8-inch layer of finished compost or wood chips to the surface of an actively composting windrow. This layer serves as a biofilter.

Runoff and Leachate Control

Control of drainage and pile leachate from a composting site is the responsibility of the composter. Water runoff is defined as direct rainfall that has moved off-site and may contain sediment, nutrients, pathogens, or organic matter from the compost operation. Pile leachate is defined as any liquid drainage from a wet pile.

Properly selecting, mixing, and managing compost materials allows control of nutrient and pathogen movement. For example, water-soluble nitrate (NO_3) is best controlled by maintaining an appropriate C:N ratio in the composting mixture. Proper management of the C:N ratio is one of the simplest and most effective ways to limit nitrate pollution from a compost site.

The water content of a pile is another management factor. Excess water, in addition to increasing the potential for odor via saturated anaerobic conditions, increases the potential for dirty runoff and pile leachate during rainfall events. If excess moisture is a concern, windrows should be oriented parallel to the slope (perpendicular to the contour) so that precipitation landing between the windrows can move freely away from the composting area. Also, a concave (dished-top) windrow shape retains water, while a convex (peaked) shape tends to shed water (see figure 3-1, page 45). To avoid standing pools of water, land slope at the site should be approximately 2–4% (2–4 feet of drop over a horizontal distance of 100 feet). Slopes over 7% are not recommended, because they move runoff water too quickly and pose driving problems. In some cases site grading may be necessary.

Ditches and berms that divert clean, upslope (run-on) water around and off the site minimize the total volume of site runoff that must be controlled (photo 4-1). These diversion channels are planted with a conservation grass/legume mix. Ideally, the composting site is graded so that direct runoff is moved off-site without creating erosion. Another method of controlling the volume of dirty runoff is to have an impervious cover or roof over compost piles, along with a clean outlet for the roof gutters. Regardless of the source, all dirty runoff from the site should be controlled, then directed to an appropriate treatment or storage system for later use.

Puddles and holding ponds for dirty runoff and leachate from the compost site can become a source of odors. In drier climates where evaporation rates are high, combined retention ponds/drying beds are the predominant method of surface water runoff protection.

Once preventive management practices are put in place to reduce the quantity of water on a site, simple treatment systems can be designed to manage and utilize compost runoff flows, including:

- land application,
- filter strips, and
- recirculation.

Land application of runoff and leachate allows organic compounds in the liquid to be adsorbed and decomposed in the soil. A vegetative filter strip (VFS) traps particles in grassed areas. Some particles in the liquid settle out, while others are filtered and adsorbed onto plants. Figure 4-1 shows a grassed filter area for treating compost pad runoff. The size of filter areas should be sufficient to provide infiltration of expected runoff from the compost pad. Recirculation involves pumping runoff water back onto the compost windrows during hot, dry weather, where organic compounds in the runoff can be recovered and decomposed.

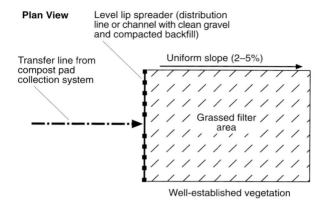

FIGURE 4-1. Grassed filter area for treating compost pad runoff

Some facilities may require additional management practices to reduce the threat of pollution, including sediment basins or treatment ponds. Sediment basins settle out solids, which include bound nutrients such as phosphorus. However, gravity settling is not likely to remove soluble nutrients or biochemical oxygen demand (BOD) as efficiently as land application (through soil adsorption and crop uptake). In treatment ponds or lagoons, microorganisms continue the decomposition process started in the compost pile, but in an aqueous system. To be effective, treatment ponds must be large enough to contain runoff from major storm events and provide an adequate residence time for microbial stabilization.

Vector Control

Vectors are animals and insect pests such as raccoons, foxes, rats, flies, birds, and mosquitoes that carry pathogens from one host to another. Dust and water can also act as vectors. Vectors are sometimes attracted to fresh compostables, and they need to be controlled for both public health and aesthetic reasons. Mosquitoes and other insects can become a problem near ponded water.

Control measures for vectors in composting operations include:
- maintaining a clean, functional site;
- promptly adding food and other vector-attractive ingredients to compost piles;
- blending fresh, putrescible organics with a carbon source or covering them with a layer of finished compost to deter flies, rodents, and birds;
- controlling ammonia production with a proper C:N ratio (ammonia is a strong attraction for flies);
- after about one week, turning and mixing piles sufficiently to promote rapid decomposition and kill any maggots just below the surface of the pile (for long-term fly control, turning and mixing intervals should be kept shorter than the fly's five- to ten-day life cycle);
- providing housing for swallows, bats, or martins (to help control mosquitoes); and
- if necessary, employing rodent-control measures (owls and hawks can help control rodents).

Dust Control

Dust has many sources on a farm composting site, including un-paved roads, unswept mixing areas, and dry materials handling. If not properly managed, dust can become a health concern for workers (see "Operator Health," page 71). Excessive dust can cause equipment overheating and increase the risk of a facility fire. Dust also traps moisture on metal surfaces, thereby promoting corrosion of equipment.

The best way to control dust is to keep materials damp (at least 35–40% moisture content). Specific dust-control methods include:

- dampening heavy traffic areas and dry piles, as necessary;
- keeping all loading and processing areas free of spilled compost, which can dry out and cause dust problems; and
- periodically cleaning dust from structural beams, light fixtures, electrical boxes, equipment, and other surfaces (even if proper dust control measures are in place).

Noise Control

The noise audible from a farm composting operation is dependent upon several factors, including loudness, frequency, distance, background noise, and individual perception. Noise is measured on a logarithmic scale in units of decibels (dB). A normal conversation generates sound levels of about 60 dBA (the "A" signifies that the measure approximately covers the human perception range). A passing heavy truck generates about 90 dBA and a quiet library about 30 dBA. An increase of 10 dBA is generally perceived by humans as "twice as loud." Sound levels decrease with distance from the source and are moderated by vegetation and terrain.

Noises from a farm compost operation can come from several sources, including:

- on-site vehicle traffic (back-up beepers, engine exhaust systems, horns, etc.);
- hammermills, tub grinders, and other high-impact equipment;
- hydraulic power units;
- generators;
- motors and gears; and
- amplified bells and alarms.

Noisy operations, such as grinding, unloading, and hauling, are often of greater concern during warmer weather when windows are open and neighbors are outside. Consequently, scheduling certain operations during the day and carefully selecting transportation routes can often reduce noise complaints. Equipment should be operated appropriately and maintained properly to reduce noise. Buffers consisting of berms, trees, and distance from other land uses are also effective controls for noise.

Safety and Accident Prevention

Most safety problems at composting sites are related to equipment. Farm managers should provide appropriate training and communicate clearly how to operate equipment and how to service it for efficiency and safety. A log of safety devices for all machines and maintenance manuals should be kept current. Printed memos and safety signs regarding proper equipment use should be posted where appropriate. Employees should be discouraged from rushing when handling and processing materials, since this is a common cause of equipment accidents.

Equipment operating manuals are one of the most important injury prevention items on the farm. All equipment manufacturers are required to clearly label a machine's operating and safety procedures. Loaders should be equipped with back-up alarms and fire extinguishers. In larger operations, windrow turners and screens can be equipped with temperature-controlled cabs to reduce worker fatigue and CB radios for instant communication.

Additional precautions must be followed when specialized windrow-turning equipment is used. Several turners contain mixing flails rotating at high speed, which should be well-shielded from human or animal contact. As the flails rotate through the compost windrow or pile, they eject stones and other foreign matter which can become dangerous projectiles. Equipment operators and other workers at the site must maintain a safe distance both around and behind operating machinery. Tub grinders should be operated fully loaded to prevent throwing of material. Locate processing equipment away from areas of public access.

Most injuries are preventable with proper training and good common sense. Initial training for employees should include basic safety tips on injury prevention and emergency response. Workers should be required to wear seat belts when operating loaders and wear safety glasses, hard hats, and ear plugs (especially when around large grinders, such as tub grinders). Additional protective gear includes particle respirators, full steel-toed and steel-shank boots, and radios.

Topics discussed at safety training meetings should include Lockout/Tagout/Blockout procedures for equipment. The objective of Lockout/Tagout procedures is to eliminate the unintentional start-up or movement of any equipment that is either being maintained or out of service. Each time a piece of equipment is "tagged out" or "locked out," it should not be operated without proper authorization. Blockout procedures refer to proper jacking and safety blocking during repairs.

Each worker should be trained for his or her specific duties and should be completely familiar with his or her assigned operation. Equipment operators must be able to recognize controls quickly and understand the response from each control. Some manufacturers provide controls with special shapes to avoid confusion during operation. Constant communication with persons working around equipment is essential so machinery can be shut down in the event of an accident. New workers should be provided thorough training regarding each area's hazards, such as blind spots and flying debris.

Operator Health

Workers need to be informed about appropriate practices and health issues related to composting. For example, particulate respirators should be provided for all workers in areas of excessive dust. Sealed, ventilated cabs on equipment should have washable or disposable filters. Workers should be given the responsibility and time to clean or change these filters regularly. Drainage facilities should be provided in work areas to remove ponded water and leachate that may contain pathogens or vectors or cause workers to slip and fall. Workers need to follow sensible precautions regarding protective clothing and equipment and treating and disinfecting cuts. Normal sanitary measures such as washing hands before touching food or eyes are important for workers.

A few individuals may be particularly sensitive to some of the organisms present in the dust from compost. The high populations of many different species of molds and fungi in an active compost pile may cause allergic-type reactions in a small percentage of sensitive individuals. Simple precautions, such as the use of particulate respirators or half-mask respirators with disposable cartridges, can help limit human exposure to these microbes. Grinding and screening equipment can also be relocated so that dominant winds blow dust and other particulate matter away from the operator.

Microorganisms dispersed through the air that affect human health are called bioaerosols. Two of the most well-known bioaerosols are *Aspergillis fumigatus* and endotoxins. *Aspergillis fumigatus*, a common fungus found in decaying organic matter and soil, is the bioaerosol of most concern because it can cause respiratory infection. This fungus is heat-tolerant and can survive the high temperatures normally found in composting. Endotoxins, which are microbial cell byproducts, can be harmful to humans and animals.

Common sources of bioaerosols include cellulose materials such as wood chips, hay, and sawdust. The three methods of transmission are inhalation, ingestion, and dermal contact. Efforts to prevent bioaerosol-related health problems should focus on reducing dust or dust exposure, assigning immunocompromised workers to activities with low exposures, and locating compost sites away from nursing homes or other sensitive areas where a potential health liability exists.

Factors that might predispose a person to infections from or allergic-type responses to bioaerosols include a weakened immune system, allergies, asthma, use of some medications such as antibiotics or adrenal cortical hormones, or a punctured eardrum. Workers with these conditions should not be assigned to exposed duties in a composting operation. If a worker develops an infection or has a negative reaction to compost, it is important to recognize the problem quickly so that it does not develop into a chronic condition.

Spills and Standing Water

Spills and standing water can be the result of seepage from piles of raw, wet feedstocks or partially processed liquid materials. They can also be caused by oversaturation of compost piles with water or by runoff from heavy rainfall events. Most liquid spills can be minimized using proper containment and handling procedures.

The best way to avoid spills in the mixing area is to immediately incorporate incoming liquid materials into the compost pile. Enough bulking agent should be added to the pile to absorb excess moisture. Always keep extra bulking agent on hand for excessively wet materials or unanticipated wet conditions. Since waterborne pollutants in compost leachate and runoff are a potential environmental hazard, these liquids must be carefully managed. Some composting operations may opt to install treatment ponds to manage the collected nutrients and pathogens. Treated liquids can be used to irrigate field crops; however, mechanized pumping systems are expensive.

Fires

Fires are rarely a problem in outdoor composting operations, since properly moistened composting material does not readily burn. However, if the compost dries out or if windrows and piles are built too large, fire becomes a possibility. In compost piles over 12 feet high, it is possible for the internal heat of the pile to initiate chemical reactions, which can lead to spontaneous combustion. Materials used as bulking agents such as chipped brush, sawdust, and so on can also be a potential fire hazard, as these materials usually do not have a high moisture content.

Attention to moisture, temperature, and pile size is the best protection against fire. As a safety precaution against fire, an adequate water supply should be available at the site. In addition, road configurations should allow access by firefighting equipment. Extra caution should be used with raw, green feedstocks that may have already started decomposing and heating. Bark chips, if given enough moisture to start biological activity, can also become extremely hot in a very short time. Large piles of coarse compost or feedstock (particle size of 4 inches and above), such as wood chips and mulch-type products, are especially susceptible to fire because of the relatively large particle size, high porosity and oxygen content, and slow biological decomposition that causes continued heat buildup, chemical oxidation, and accelerated pile drying.

Fires that occur in stored materials, equipment, or buildings should be handled according to practiced emergency procedures. In case of fire, operators should know how to:

- disconnect power to the affected area,
- notify local fire officials,
- evacuate the area, and
- attempt to extinguish the fire safely.

To extinguish a pile fire, burning compost or mulch should be spread out and soaked with water. A burning pile should be pulled apart, because water will not penetrate into a dry pile; rather, it will run off the dry surface. Dry compost should be spread out to approximately a 1-foot depth or less. When you have pulled away all unburned material and isolated the area that's smoldering, then apply water generously.

CHAPTER 5: Composting Livestock and Poultry Mortalities

This chapter outlines the procedures for composting animal mortalities. Planning, construction, and management practices are explained for three different mortality composting systems: (1) minicomposters, (2) two-bin systems, and (3) composting of catastrophic mortalities. At the end of the chapter, the following environmental and regulatory issues are presented: groundwater and surface water protection, biosecurity, odor, insects, scavengers, and utilization of animal mortality compost.

NOTE: *Most of the information presented in this chapter is taken from the paper "Composting Animal Mortality," written by Herbert L. Brodie and Lewis E. Carr, Extension Agricultural Engineers at the University of Maryland at College Park. Figures and examples are from University of Maryland Cooperative Extension Service Fact Sheet 537, "Composting Dead Birds," written by Dennis W. Murphy, Extension Poultry Science Specialist, and Lewis E. Carr. Other contributing authors and source materials for this chapter are incorporated in the reference section on page 115.*

Traditional mortality handling methods include burial at the farm or at landfills, incineration, and renderer pickup. Composting mortality is gaining popularity because it is cost effective, environmentally sound, biosecure, and easy. Composting decomposes mortalities to a useful farm product (soil amendment) without the production of objectionable odors or the attraction of flies or scavenging birds and animals. Composting avoids putting mortalities in the soil, where groundwater contamination is a risk.

Although mortality composting was initially developed for broiler chicken farms, it has been successfully used to handle swine, cattle, and horse carcasses of mature size as well as sheep, fish, dairy calves, and other animals. Mortality composting has also been used for catastrophic events where an entire flock of chickens might be lost to disease or stress, or a group of cows might be killed by a lightning strike. Some landfills compost deer and other animals killed along roadways. The U.S. Environmental Protection Agency considers farm composting of livestock manure and poultry carcasses as a best management practice to reduce agricultural nonpoint source pollution.

Compost Process for Animal Mortalities

Composting animal mortalities is a process of burying carcasses within a drier amendment such as poultry litter, straw bedding, spoiled silage, leaves, sawdust, or other compostables. Sawmill sawdust has been shown to be a good material in which to compost dead animals. Composting develops temperatures that slowly cook and decompose animal tissues while eliminating pathogens and parasites. The process may require as little as several days for small birds to six or more months for mature cattle. The compost resulting from the process can be field spread as a manure. Many provinces and states have or are developing regulations making composting a suitable means of mortality management in the United States and Canada.

The biological process of composting animal mortalities is similar to the process occurring in the composting of other organic materials. In mortality composting, the needed parameters of air, water, nutrients, and carbon must be balanced to initiate the compost process and produce enough heat to provide for pathogen reduction in the mass. These conditions are obtained by an optimum mix of compostable materials where:

1. the mortalities (animal carcasses) provide nitrogen and water, and

2. materials such as sawdust, straw, paper, corn stalks, and other bulky, fibrous materials provide carbon and porosity.

Ingredients

Sawdust is an ideal medium because of its small particle size, which allows maximum contact with carcass tissue while retaining good pile structure and porosity. Livestock bedding, poultry litter removed from animal growing areas, and screened solids from manure liquid-solids separators can all be used as long as the material is not saturated with moisture. Residential organic materials such as leaves or shredded paper mixed with green grass will also heat well. New mixtures of compost ingredients can often be supplemented with old compost to reduce the need for sawdust and straw. However, in order to maintain adequate levels of carbon for the composting microbes, new material should account for at least half of the mix requirement.

Moisture

A very important factor in mortality composting is the moisture content of the compost mix. Too little moisture promotes dehydration, which preserves carcass tissues. Too much moisture leads to foul odors and contaminating leachate. The moisture content of the compost mix should be approximately 40–50% — a squeezed handful of compost mix should leave wetness on the palm but not drip. The animal carcasses usually provide sufficient additional water in relation to their size and quantity. Because large animal carcasses provide considerable water, the starting compost mix can be slightly dry. However, the animal hair should be wetted. Small animals loaded a few at a time add little water for composting; therefore, the mix may need additional water. Old and dehydrated carcasses will require additional water.

Management

Composting mortalities are managed in a static pile or bin. The mix is turned (for aeration and mixing) once or twice during the active compost period and prior to placement in a curing pile. During active composting, the animal carcasses are cooked and then decomposed. The heat produced within the compost pile is sufficient to kill common pathogens. The total time required for composting ranges from two to twelve months, depending on animal size and the rate of composting (colder climates and larger animals require more time).

Before composting animal mortalities, you should practice basic composting procedures. Valuable experience can be gained with backyard-sized compost bins using yard trimmings or animal manures without mortalities. Once basic procedures have been understood and mastered, on-farm mortality composting will have a much higher chance of success.

Mortality Composting Systems

Mortality composting can take place in:

- small bins called minicomposters,
- dedicated composter buildings,
- temporary open bins fashioned from large bales of hay or straw, and
- windrows or piles on paved or compacted soil surfaces.

Perhaps the simplest form of mortality composting is bin composting, which is actually a form of in-vessel composting. Bin composting (including minicomposters) is readily adaptable to poultry farms. Minicomposters are managed with a pitchfork and shovel, while larger bins and piles require the use of a tractor bucket loader for moving and mixing material. On-farm windrow composting is also well-suited to poultry and other mortalities.

Another form of mortality composting not covered in this guide is the use of rotating drums. These in-vessel systems have shown good preliminary results in Texas for composting poultry carcasses, dairy manure, and other agricultural residues (photo 1g).

Minicomposters

Minicomposters are useful for poultry, piglets, rabbits, and other small animals. Minicomposters can range from simple boxes made of pallets to constructed bins of wood and plastic mesh. The dimensions must be sufficient to allow heat retention in the mass of composting material. Minimum dimensions are approximately 3 feet in height and length on any side. A minicomposter of this size will accept a maximum of 30 pounds of mortalities per day and can process a cumulative total of up to 600 pounds. Multiple bins can be constructed for greater amounts of mortalities.

Minicomposters can be placed in the animal growing area because they are almost odorless and, when properly operated, are biosecure. Locating the minicomposter in a warm area protected from wind will help retain pile heat and increase the rate of composting.

The process is started by layering compost ingredients in the minicomposter. A proven volumetric ratio recipe of 2 broiler litter: 1 fluffed straw in 6-inch layers has worked very well on broiler farms and produces a C:N ratio of approximately 18–20. Where poultry litter is not available, experiment with other materials before composting mortalities (sawdust has proven to be a good alternative). Before adding dead animals, the bin should be layered two-thirds full with litter and straw. Adjust moisture by adding water as the layers are being formed. The intent is to have a compost mixture that rapidly heats and is brought up to a temperature of 95°F before the dead animals are placed in the bin. A compost thermometer (figure 3-4, page 51) is necessary to determine when the bin is ready for loading and to make sure that the temperature is maintained throughout the process.

The carcasses are buried in the center of the heating compost with a minimum of 6 inches of insulating compost cover on all sides, above and below the mortalities. For chickens, the following procedure can be used, based on the volume of birds to be treated:

1. Dig a hole in the compost large enough to hold three times the volume of birds to be buried.
2. Cover the bottom of the hole with straw equal to one-third the volume of the birds.

3. Cover the straw with dry broiler litter equal to three-fourths the volume of the birds.

4. Place the birds on the litter.

5. Pour water over the birds equal to one-third the volume of the birds.

6. Cover the birds with litter equal to three-fourths the volume of the birds.

7. Smooth off the top of the compost to finish filling the hole.

Birds can be loaded daily in this manner, and their soft tissues will be completely decomposed in 48 hours. Similar procedures are used with other animal species and compostable materials.

When the minicomposter bin is filled, and at least seven days after the last addition of carcasses, the unit can be disassembled and the compost removed to be disposed of or stored as manure. One-third to one-half of a bin of compost can be used in place of new materials for the start of a new compost cycle.

Two-Bin System

A two-bin system, made up of a primary and secondary treatment bin, is used when mortality rates exceed the capacity of minicomposters or the weight of individual animals is greater than 30 pounds. Treatment bins can be designed of wood, masonry, or, for temporary construction, a material such as hay bales. The size of the compost bin should be a compromise between:

- the number and size of the animals composted and
- the size of the equipment used to move the compost.

Under normal rates of mortality, smaller bins allow better management. Primary treatment bins about 5 feet long by 8 feet wide by 5 feet high are suitable for animals less than 330 pounds (figure 5-1). Bins of this size also allow entrance with the average farm tractor bucket. The height of primary and secondary bins should not exceed 5 feet. The total number of treatment bins required for the farm is based on the need for 1 cubic foot of primary bin and 1 cubic foot of secondary bin for each pound of mortality expected per day (see example calculation on page 78).

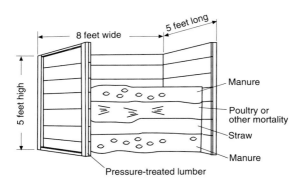

FIGURE 5-1. Primary treatment bin in two-bin system

Problem: A broiler flock of 93,000 birds has an expected maximum mortality rate of 0.25% per day. The average live weight of each bird at market age is 4.5 pounds. How many primary and secondary bins are required to compost the expected daily mortality?

Solution: First, determine the number of primary bins required. The number of primary treatment bins needed is equal to the total primary capacity divided by the length, multiplied by the width, multiplied by the height of each primary bin. Assume that a primary bin length of 5 feet and a width of 7 feet will accommodate the existing farm loader. Assume a bin height of 5 feet.

Primary
capacity = 93,000 birds x (0.25% mortality/day) x (4.5 lbs/bird)

    = 1,050 lbs/day

The number of primary bins required is:

Primary
bins = 1,050 ÷ (L x W x H) = 1,050 cu ft* ÷ (5 ft x 7 ft x 5 ft)

    = 6 primary bins

Next, determine the size and shape of the secondary bin(s). Assume a width of 7 feet and a height of 5 feet. Solve for length, as follows:

Total length of
secondary bin(s) = 1,050 cu ft* ÷ (7 ft x 5 ft) = 30 ft

* The total number of bins required for the farm is based on the need of 1 cubic foot of primary bin and 1 cubic foot of secondary bin for each pound of mortality expected per day.

Ideally, bins should be constructed on an impervious surface and covered with a roof (photo 5-1). Roofing allows improved moisture control in both wet and dry weather. An impervious floor allows use in all weather conditions and makes it easier to identify leachate caused by mismanagement. For temporary use, three-sided bins can be constructed of large bales of hay or straw. The bales can be placed to provide one continuous large bin or multiple bins. One advantage of temporary bale bins is that they can be placed directly in the field where the compost will eventually be applied.

Animal carcasses are loaded into the primary bin of the two-bin system *before heating begins* (figure 5-1, page 77). Additional carcasses are loaded in layers and covered with compost ingredients until the bin is full. Be sure to keep carcasses away from the edges to reduce access by scavenging animals. Small carcasses can be placed side by side in layers 8–10 inches thick, with 6 inches of compost mix between and around each layer. Add water, if necessary, as the layers are being constructed. Finish with a 12-inch-thick top cover of compost mix. Table 5-1 presents a sample compost recipe for composting dead birds using manure and straw.

Animals weighing less than 300 pounds can be composted whole with no preparation. Larger animals may require opened thoracic and abdominal cavities, opened viscera, and sliced large muscle masses. Animal carcasses should not be cut into very small pieces (see "Procedures for Large Animals" on page 80).

TABLE 5-1. Sample compost recipe for composting poultry mortality

	Manure	Dead birds	Straw	Total	Weighted average
Volume proportion	2.0	1.0	1.0		
Weight proportion	1.5	1.0	0.1		
Pounds	1,500	1,000	100	2,600	
Percentage	57.7	38.5	3.8	100	
Percentage of moisture	30	70	10		44.6
C:N ratio	25	5	85		19.6

Source: Sussman, 1984.

During active composting, animal tissues are cooked and then rapidly decomposed. The compost temperature starts to decline seven to ten days after the last carcasses were added to the bin. The compost mass is then turned for aeration by moving the compost to a secondary bin. When moving the pile to the second bin, make sure that any exposed animal parts are fully covered with at least 12 inches of compost. Animal carcasses are essentially reduced to bone after an additional ten to thirty days.

Bin systems using sawdust can be recharged with new carcasses as long as most of the sawdust particles are identifiable and fresh sawdust is added to maintain the original volume. If a majority of the sawdust particles appear composted, place two-thirds of the compost in a curing pile or manure storage shed for a minimum of thirty days before field spreading. Add the remaining one-third of the compost in a mix of new materials for recharging the bin.

At the University of Maryland, approximately 3,000 pounds of swine mortalities (piglets, afterbirth, sows, and boars) were composted in a 200-cubic-foot bin of sawdust over a period of fourteen months, without changing the sawdust. The bin was sporadically filled as mortality occurred and continually maintained temperatures in excess of 130–150°F.

In the two-bin system, the control of pathogens is maximized when the entire mass exceeds 130°F for at least three consecutive days. Although some large bones may remain, the combination of the cooking process, rapid decomposition, and compost cover provides good control of flies and odor. As with minicomposters, a thermometer is a necessary management tool for the two-bin system. Figure 5-2 illustrates a multicompartmentalized, two-bin design that includes a roof, a concrete floor, and rot-resistant materials.

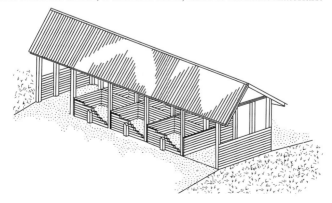

FIGURE 5-2. Maryland freestanding, two-stage composter

Procedures for Large Animals

Large-animal composting is simply the burial of the animal carcass in a compostable medium. Although silage, chopped straw, and other readily available materials can be used, sawdust is preferred because it is very absorbent, and the small particles can come into good contact with the animal tissue. Because large-animal mortality does not usually occur on a daily basis, a design loading density of 10 pounds or less of animal per cubic foot of sawdust has proven successful.

The animal carcasses must be placed on and covered with a minimum of 12 inches of sawdust. The sawdust base acts as a sponge for fluids, while the cover acts as a biofilter to capture odor. The sawdust base should be increased to 24 inches deep for mature cattle and larger animals. Usually the volume of sawdust (or other material) required to support and cover a large animal exceeds the minimum loading density outlined above.

Large animal carcasses over 300 pounds may require opened thoracic and abdominal cavities, opened viscera, and sliced large muscle masses to accelerate the compost process and prevent possible explosion of intestinal cavities. The carcass should be placed in the composting medium backbone down with legs spread so that fluids do not readily drain and the cover material can contact the opened body cavities. The animal hair or fur should be wetted with water before covering with the compost mix. Refer to state or provincial regulations, if they exist.

Compost bins or piles can be filled in batches, or animal carcasses can be placed in the bin or pile as needed until the maximum loading density is reached. The compost is turned (for mixing) about three months after the maximum loading density is reached, regardless of when loading started. The last animal placed must be given adequate treatment time. After turning, any exposed animal parts must be fully covered with compost. After three or four months of additional composting, the material can be field spread. Times may increase during the cold months. Odor should be unnoticeable if the process has been left undisturbed and a deep compost cover has been maintained.

Although some large bones remain in the compost, they lose structure and are easily broken in the spreading process. At the University of Maryland, the only bones remaining in a dairy cow carcass left in a static compost pile for one and a half years were large ball ends, which were easily crumbled.

Although bins are preferred for containment, steep-sided peaked compost piles can be equally effective. The location of discrete piles should be high, dry, easily accessible, and away from surface waterways. Compost made from straw, leaves, or materials other than sawdust may require a tarp cover or roof to shed rain. An added advantage of using sawdust is that, when steeply piled, it forms a surface crust that sheds rain and prevents saturation.

Composting Catastrophic Mortalities

Catastrophic mortalities are caused by uncontrollable events, such as power failure, flooding, disease, etc., that cause many animals to die in a short period of time. Occasionally, a producer is under order of a state or federal government agency to destroy animals to halt the spread of disease. In these situations, carcasses should be handled quickly in an environmentally sound manner to reduce the risk of disease, odor, vermin, scavengers, and water pollution.

The composting of catastrophic mortalities is not much different from other composting methods, except that catastrophic mortalities usually occur on a larger scale and at unexpected times. Livestock managers should be prepared for such an event by keeping on hand the proper type and volume of feedstock materials for composting catastrophic mortalities.

Because of the volume of carcasses to be composted, catastrophic mortalities are most often composted in open-air static windrows without enclosed bins or dividing walls. In general, the compost windrow should be no more than 12 feet wide at the base and no more than 6–7 feet high. Windrows can be extended to any length to accommodate the volume of mortality or to fit the site. They should be located on high, dry ground away from surface waterways.

Animals raised on bedding or litter can be composted in the bedding or litter where they were housed if the whole population is involved and if adequate space is available. The compost process will kill disease organisms in the bedding, assist in the control of disease, and treat the mortalities. Both small and large animals can be layered in the compost mix. A generic method of composting catastrophic mortalities is outlined below.

Materials needed for composting catastrophic mortalities include:
- a well-drained compost site 150 feet from streams, ditches, poultry houses, and farm neighbors (can use a manure storage shed or other covered structure, if available);
- source of feedstock materials (stockpiled throughout the year);
- front-end loader;
- 6-mil plastic (optional — to collect long-term pile leachate);
- a responsible person to manage the operation; and
- a thermometer with a 36-inch probe.

Basic process requirements for composting catastrophic mortalities are:
- carbon — sawdust, broiler litter, cornstalks, straw, bedding, etc.
- nitrogen — carcass and fecal matter in litter or bedding
- moisture — 40–55%
- proper aeration — through proper pile construction (see below).

The following procedure can be used to construct a static pile or windrow for composting catastrophic mortalities:
1. Select a proper site for composting (include adequate space for loading).
2. Place a layer of 6-mil plastic on the ground 10–12 feet wide and the total length of the windrow or pile. (Step 2 is optional if composted material is land applied immediately.)
3. Place carbon material such as broiler litter as a base, approximately 12–18 inches deep.
4. Place carcasses on top of the base, 12 inches from the edge of the base material and not more than 8–10 inches thick [e.g., using large broilers two birds thick, the approximate ratio by volume would be 2:1 (litter:carcasses)].
5. Apply water to thoroughly wet feathers or fur. Dissect larger animals (over 300 pounds) as described in "Procedures for Large Animals," page 80.
6. Place a 6–8-inch cover layer of carbon material over carcasses.
7. Repeat layers as necessary, until the pile or windrow is 5–6 feet high (figure 5-3, page 82).

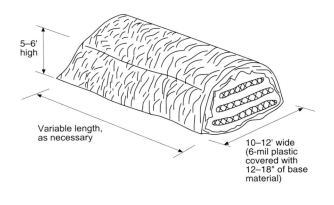

5–6' high

Variable length, as necessary

10–12' wide (6-mil plastic covered with 12–18" of base material)

Animal carcass layer (10–12" thick, wetted, and covered with 6–8" of carbon material)

FIGURE 5-3. Carcass layering for windrow composting of animal mortality

After four to five days, the temperature at the core of the pile should reach approximately 145°F. After about ten to fourteen days, the pile should be reduced to about three quarters of its original volume, mainly due to decomposition of soft carcass tissue. At this time the pile can be turned, but make sure to keep carcasses covered. After mixing, pile core temperatures should quickly rise to between 140° and 150°F for the next seven to fourteen days. When core temperatures decline again, turn the pile with care, keeping bones and hard tissues covered. When sustained lower core temperatures (below 145°F) are noted, and before the compost is land applied or stored under plastic, the compost should be cured for approximately two months. If the above guidelines are followed, composting of catastrophic mortalities can be done without the environmental and health nuisances caused by odors, flies, disease, and black-liquid leachate.

Environmental and Regulatory Issues

Many governmental agencies responsible for mortality treatment are forming or changing regulations to allow for mortality composting as a recommended practice. Some jurisdictions have no regulations specific to mortality composting but regulate on a complaint basis under nuisance or other environmental laws.

Many jurisdictions require permits that may dictate specific procedures, locations, or structures for mortality composting. Some states provide cost-share money as an incentive for farmers to construct approved compost structures. Most jurisdictions rely on agricultural agencies and universities for guidance. Maryland and Ohio require some degree of approved training for mortality compost operators. All jurisdictions require adherence to water and air quality regulations for mortality treatment.

Groundwater and Surface Water Protection

As with all farm activities, animal mortality composting should be done with an awareness of potential impacts on water quality. Poorly constructed or maintained compost piles can produce leachate that may carry pathogens to nearby water systems.

Compost piles that are roofed or covered help limit leachate caused by saturating rains. However, steep-sided piles of sawdust also provide excellent shedding of rain. Piles or bins made with absorbent materials reduce the potential for leachate by absorbing internal fluids from the carcass. Animal loading densities less than the maximum will ensure further capture and control of leachate and ensure that the process around the carcass remains aerobic.

Piles located outside should be on high, compacted, dry ground away from surface waterways. Windrows should be shaped to shed water (see figure 3-1 on page 45) and oriented on sloped land to run parallel to the slope, so surface runoff is not captured by the compost. A buffer of growing vegetation should exist between the compost site and surface water drainage pathways (see "Runoff and Leachate Control," page 68).

Biosecurity

A primary concern with concentrated livestock operations is the spread of infectious disease among the animals. Because pathogenic organisms may be transported by people, animals, vehicles, and wind, diligent management is required. Under disease conditions, it is preferable to keep all animal mortalities on the farm rather than risk spreading disease to some other location.

Composting carcasses is a good biosecurity measure, because pathogenic organisms common to animal production can be killed by exposure to temperatures between 130° and 150°F (see "Controlling Process Time and Temperature," page 47). For optimum disease control, compost processes should occur as described for the two-bin system (i.e., the entire mass should exceed 130°F for at least three consecutive days). Proper monitoring of pile temperatures and timely turning ensure that sufficient temperatures are reached and that composting piles remain aerobic (see "Monitoring and Recordkeeping," page 49).

Surveys for microbes in poultry and swine mortality composting systems indicate that no deleterious pathogens survive when systems are maintained in the recommended manner. However, some pathogenic organisms may not be effectively controlled by compost process temperatures. Consequently, as a positive biosecurity measure, compost produced from diseased or suspect animals can be buried or incinerated. In addition, mortality compost areas should be fenced to prevent access by other farm animals.

Odor, Insects, and Scavengers

Almost no odor is released from a correctly mixed and loaded mortality composter. Odor is an indication that the process is not being managed properly. Factors usually responsible for odor generation are:

- excessive carcass loading (too much nitrogen),
- too low or high moisture content,
- too little oxygen, or
- lack of adequate cover completely surrounding the carcass.

Odor can also occur outside of the compost pile from a partially decaying animal carcass that has not been fully incorporated into the pile in a timely manner. Monitoring compost temperature is a good way to avoid odor. Temperatures that are too low or that fail to increase after loading indicate a problem with the process and forewarn of pending odor (see "Troubleshooting," page 52).

The heat produced in minicomposters and bin composters, combined with proper turning of the compost, prevents the development of insect larvae. Adding a dry layer of composted material on the top of a bin or pile reduces fly access for egg laying. Other insects normally found in decaying woody products may be present in the compost pile at some point during the process and should not be considered pests (see figure 3-2, page 47).

Compost bins or piles that are correctly mixed and adequately covered with a blanket of compost mix to capture odor will not attract vermin and scavengers. Trials of mortality composting at the University of Maryland in areas frequented by dogs, fox, buzzards, and raccoons showed no sign of disturbance. A similar experience was found at the University of Massachusetts mortality compost sites. However, if a compost pile is turned and all carcass parts are not completely covered or a new layer of compost mix is not placed over the pile, then a scent attractive to scavengers may be released. Piled carcasses that are not immediately incorporated into a compost pile or bin will also attract scavengers. Composting mortalities should be inspected regularly and covered with additional compost mix if there is evidence of scavenger entry.

Utilizing Mortality Compost

The conversion of animal carcasses and other materials into bacterial biomass and humus produces a beneficial fertilizer and soil amendment. Nevertheless, because of biosecurity concerns, it is recommended that mortality compost be used solely for soil amendment on the land where the animals were produced. In addition, mortality compost should not be used as animal bedding or feed supplement or given to others for use off the farm.

Mortality compost can be land spread with or as manure and should be included in the farm nutrient management plan. The nutrients, humus, and soil-amending properties in a mortality compost make it a valuable byproduct to a livestock enterprise. Composted poultry mortalities, for example, provide a slower and more sustained release of nitrogen than the built-up litter on which the birds were raised. This is caused by the conversion during composting of mineral nitrogen to an organic form. Table 5-2 compares the nutrients of a built-up litter with those of poultry mortality compost.

TABLE 5-2. Nutrients in built-up (12-flock) litter and dead bird compost

Analysis	Built-up litter	Dead bird compost
Moisture	21.00%	46.10%
Primary macronutrients:	Dry basis (wet basis[a])	Dry basis (wet basis[a])
Nitrogen, percentage	4.15 (3.28)	2.20 (1.19)
Phosphorus (P_2O_5), percentage	3.80 (3.00)	3.27 (1.76)
Potash (K_2O), percentage	2.85 (2.25)	2.39 (1.29)
Secondary macronutrients:		
Calcium, percentage	1.70 (1.34)	1.33 (0.72)
Magnesium, percentage	0.91 (0.72)	0.82 (0.44)
Sulfur, percentage	0.51 (0.40)	0.40 (0.21)
Micronutrients:		
Manganese, parts per million	208.00 (164.32)	122.00 (65.76)
Zinc, parts per million	331.00 (261.49)	245.00 (132.06)
Copper, parts per million	205.00 (161.95)	197.00 (106.18)

Source of data: Murphy and Carr, 1991.

[a] Wet or "as is" basis can be determined from procedures outlined on pages 33–34 of this field guide.

CHAPTER 6: Compost Utilization on the Farm

This chapter presents some important characteristics and benefits of farm composts, as well as a brief overview of the most common uses of compost on the farm. At the end of the chapter is a brief section on compost application designed to aid farmers in managing field applications.

Compost Characteristics

Compost characteristics such as stability, organic matter content, pH, water-holding capacity, and plant nutrient content are of keen interest. The presence of phytotoxic (plant-harmful) materials, such as soluble salts, volatile organic acids, and heavy metals, impedes seed germination and root growth. Compost characteristics such as bulk density, moisture content, particle size, and texture influence how a compost is handled.

Starting the composting process with appropriate raw materials is the best way to ensure a good finished compost. If composting has been poorly managed with regard to unwanted materials in feedstocks, it will be difficult to achieve a good compost quality. The quality of finished compost also depends on storage time and conditions. Compost that has aged three to four months following curing will tend to have a lower pH, higher bulk density, finer texture, and higher concentration of nitrate-nitrogen.

!!**CAUTION:** Compost piles that become anaerobic, or sour, are likely to develop odors and contain alcohols and VOAs (volatile organic acids). Anaerobic byproducts are detrimental to plants. The application of anaerobic compost to sensitive plants or as a mulch over shallow-rooted plants will kill the plants almost instantly. A compost that has become anaerobic can easily be identified by its odor and acidic pH, which may be near 3.0. This situation can be corrected by stacking the compost in smaller piles, thereby allowing the material to "air out" and compost further.

Listed below are some important characteristics of farm compost.

Organic Matter Content

Compost is a significant source of organic matter, which is an important supplier of carbon. Organic matter improves soil and plant efficiency by improving soil physical properties, providing a source of energy to beneficial organisms, and enhancing the reservoir of soil nutrients. A productive soil should have at least 3–4% organic matter. The organic content of a soil can be built up slowly through repeated applications of compost or other organic materials. The organic content of composts ranges from about 35% to 70% (the preferred range is 50–60%).

Nutrient Content

While some benefits from compost application are derived from its organic matter and soil-improving qualities, compost also provides major nutrients such as nitrogen, phosphorus, and potassium for plant growth. Nutrient managers use the measured nutrient content of applied soil amendments to adjust agronomic practices in an effort to optimize effectiveness and minimize the risk of pollution.

Stability

Stability, a measure of the stage of compost decomposition, is solely a function of biological activity. Stability can be quantified by measuring respiration via oxygen uptake or carbon dioxide release. Compost stability is an important specification because of its effect on the availability of nutrients for growing plants. A stable compost provides some measure of plant nutrition, while an unstable compost demands nitrogen and oxygen from the soil. Finished composts are usually rated as moderately stable to very stable.

Pathogens and Weed Seeds

It is important that compost be free of plant pathogens. When animal manures are used as compost feedstock, the pathogens present may result in increased risk of disease transmission to animals or humans. However, if a pile is properly mixed and given enough time to attain thorough heating, the temperatures attained during active composting will normally be sufficient to destroy most on-farm pathogens and weed seeds (See "Controlling Process Time and Temperature," page 47).

Particle Size and Texture

The particle size and texture of compost or soil are determined by the size of the dominant particles in the mixture. A fine texture indicates uniformly small particles, while a coarse texture refers to uniformly large particles. A compost that does not have a uniform texture may not be biologically stable throughout. Consequently, particle size and texture can be used as indicators of product stability. Particle size and texture may also be used to determine product usability for specific applications, including mechanical performance during field application. The particle size and texture of a compost are determined by the size of the final screen. Most composts have a finished particle size under 1 inch. Composts for horticultural use usually pass either the ½-inch or ⅜-inch screen size.

pH

Assuming that all other conditions for growth are suitable, specific plants flourish when grown at their optimum soil pH. To estimate the effect of an added compost on soil or growing media pH, the pH of the compost must be known. Composts are typically slightly alkaline (pH 7.0–8.0) but may range from pH 5.0 to 8.5. The pH of a finished compost should fall between 5.5 and 8.0.

Water-Holding Capacity

Water-holding capacity is a measure of the ability of a mass such as compost or soil to hold water. In drier climates, water-holding capacity can be used to estimate the effect of compost on reducing irrigation or reducing crop water requirements. Water-holding capacity is determined as the ratio of water-filled pore space divided by the total volume of the compost or soil. For many composts, water-holding capacities range from 75% to 200%. The preferred range is 100% or greater.

Moisture Content

The moisture content of a compost, measured as the percent weight of water relative to total compost weight, has an important impact on product handling. Because moisture content affects bulk density, it is directly related to transportation costs. In addition, moisture content affects the potential for dust generation from a compost, which is an important health consideration (see "Operator Health," page 71). Typically, the threshold for dust formation is 35% moisture or less. Although finished composts can range from 35% to 60% moisture, the preferred range is 40–45%.

Bulk Density

Bulk density refers to the total wet weight of a material relative to its total volume. A common unit of measurement for compost is pounds per cubic yard (lbs/cu yd). Bulk density is an important unit of measurement, because it directly affects transportation and storage costs. Typical compost bulk densities range from approximately 700 lbs/cu yd to 1,400 lbs/cu yd. Bulk density is strongly affected by moisture content, with wetter materials having a higher bulk density. The preferred range is from 800 lbs/cu yd to 1,000 lbs/cu yd.

Seed Germination and Plant Growth Response

Seed germination and plant growth evaluation means using seeds or seedlings to verify a compost's ability to support plant growth. Normally, growth response is used to determine whether a compost mixture will negatively affect seed germination and root growth. Compost must satisfactorily pass seed germination and plant growth response tests (see "Sampling and Laboratory Testing," page 48).

Soluble Salt Content

Soluble salt content is reported in units of decisiemens per meter (dS/m). Excessive soluble salt content in a compost/soil mixture can prevent or delay seed germination and proper root growth, especially in salt-sensitive plants. The normal range of soluble salts in finished compost is 1–30 dS/m, but it is usually close to 10 dS/m. In general, the preferred soluble salt content is 5 dS/m or less, but for many horticultural applications the finished compost/soil blend should be below 3 dS/m. Existing soluble salt levels in a soil should also be considered, since they may have an impact on potential compost application.

Trace Elements

Trace elements in a compost such as copper, molybdenum, zinc, and nickel are required by plant enzymes at certain levels to support biochemical activity and maintain healthy plant growth. Crops grown on soils that have been depleted of one or more of these trace elements respond favorably to fertilizer supplements or proper compost mixtures. However, if a trace element is overapplied and the concentration in the soil becomes excessive, plant phytotoxicity can occur. Excessive concentrations of certain trace elements (called heavy metals) can be toxic to animals, including humans. When farm-generated compost is used as a soil amendment, human toxicity is unlikely.

Inerts

Inert materials such as plastics, rocks, and metal objects are undesirable in a compost. If land applied, these materials can remain in the soil for years. Inerts greater than $\frac{3}{16}$ inch (4 millimeters) can be removed by screening. However, the best way to eliminate inerts from a compost product is by keeping them out of the original source material from the beginning.

Table 6-1 lists compost quality guidelines for selected end uses, including as potting media, a top dressing (for turf), and a soil amendment.

Farm Use of Compost

Three main reasons for using compost in the production of agronomic, horticultural, and silvicultural crops are:

1. For soil improvement — to amend certain physical characteristics of the soil, such as infiltration rate, water-holding capacity, and tilth, as well as to increase the population and diversity of the soil microbial community;
2. For fertilizer — for specific nutrients such as nitrogen, phosphorus, potassium, or trace elements;
3. To add humus — for increased soil organic matter content. The effect of a compost on soil humus depends on the type of compost used. For example, well-prepared bark compost is highly recommended for raising soil humus content.

Compost is a lightweight and relatively stable form of organic matter that reduces a soil's bulk density while increasing fertility. Compost can help replenish humus and soil nutrients. Adding compost to soils improves aeration and drainage of dense soils and water-holding capacity and aggregation of sandy soils. Compost also increases a soil's exchange capacity (that is, its ability to absorb nutrients). Compost also increases the activity, populations, and diversity of soil microbes and the availability of trace elements over a wider range of pHs. Since composts tend to have a near-neutral pH, they will raise the pH of acid soils but do little to lower the pH of alkaline soils. Although the biological benefits of compost are not fully understood, compost is known to contain certain naturally occurring fungicides and beneficial organisms that improve soil biology and suppress disease-causing organisms.

!!CAUTION: When using compost for the first time in a specific application, or when using a specific type or source of compost for the first time, the compost should be tested on a small scale. A soil test is strongly suggested. It should be understood that all compost products, climatic conditions, crop requirements, and field situations are different and may require specific recommendations from experts familiar with those specific field situations. Also, be aware that states may have specific regulations regarding compost utilization. [Above recommendations were taken from The Composting Council's *Field Guide to Compost Use* (1996), which is listed in the reference section at the back of this book.]

As a Source of Nutrients and Soil Amendment for Field Crops

In principle, compost can be used for any kind of agricultural field crop. Compost can be used in combination with manure applications or when turning under a green crop. If soil moisture conditions permit, it is best to apply manure compost during the autumn

TABLE 6-1. Example of compost quality guidelines based on end use

Characteristic		Quality guidelines End use of compost			
	Potting grade	Potting media amendment grade[a]	Top dressing grade	Soil amendment grade[a]
Recommended uses	As a growing medium without additional blending	For formulating growing media for potted crops with a pH of 7.2 or below	Primarily for topdressing turf	Improvement of agricultural soils, restoration of disturbed soils, establishment and maintenance of landscape plantings with pH of 7.2 or below
Color	Dark brown to black	Dark brown to black	Dark brown to black	Dark brown to black
Odor	Should have good, earthy odor	Should have no objectionable odor	Should have no objectionable odor	Should have no objectionable odor
Particle size	Less than 1/2 inch	Less than 1/2 inch	Less than 1/4 inch	Less than 3/4 inch
pH	5.0–7.6	Range should be identified	Range should be identified	Range should be identified
Soluble salt concentration (mmhos per centimeter)	Less than 2.5	Less than 10	Less than 5	Less than 20
Foreign materials	Should not contain more than 1% by dry weight of combined glass, plastic, and other foreign particles 1/8–1/2 inch	Should not contain more than 1% by dry weight of combined glass, plastic, and other foreign particles 1/8–1/2 inch	Should not contain more than 1% by dry weight of combined glass, plastic, and other foreign particles 1/8–1/2 inch	Should not contain more than 1% by dry weight of combined glass, plastic, and other foreign particles
Heavy metals	Should not exceed EPA standards for unrestricted use	Should not exceed EPA standards for unrestricted use	Should not exceed EPA standards for unrestricted use	Should not exceed EPA standards for unrestricted use

[a] For crops requiring a pH of 6.5 or greater, use lime-fortified product. Lime-fortified soil amendment grade should have a soluble salt concentration less than 30 mmhos per centimeter.

and spring. When used as a fertilizer, compost provides a slow release of nutrients. Some composted materials such as manure may be rich in phosphorus, which can increase the risk of surface water degradation if not properly managed. Other on-farm composted products contain low levels of phosphorus but are rich in potassium. All land-applied nutrients, but especially nitrogen and phosphorus, must be carefully managed to protect water quality.

Compost applications used to increase the productivity of an agricultural soil should be based on soil test results and crop needs. When determining compost application rates based on crop needs, it is important to remember that only a portion of the nitrogen in the compost is available for plant growth during the first year. The remainder of organic nitrogen becomes available (through mineralization) in succeeding years. Consequently, in crops that require large amounts of nitrogen, supplemental application of mineral fertilizers may be necessary (see "Application Rates," page 92, and sidebar, page 93).

As a soil amendment for field crops (to maintain organic matter, tilth, and fertility), farm compost can be land applied before planting. A less mature compost can be applied as long as sufficient time is given for additional stabilization between application and planting; however, caution must be used. Although the soil provides some stabilization and buffering, a lack of compost maturity frequently causes problems.

For Disease Suppression in Horticultural Production

There is increasing evidence that enhanced microbial activity in the soil from the use of compost increases the mineralization of nitrogen and also provides suppression of diseases and insects. Annual application rates of 1.5–10 dry tons per acre as broadcast or band applications are being used to suppress diseases and destructive soilborne nematodes in certain vegetable crops such as lettuce, cabbage, and snap beans. Compost has also been shown to be effective in promoting the growth and yields of cucurbits (a gourd) in nematode-infested soils. Potting soils containing composted broiler litter, dairy manure, and steer/horse manure have been found to be suppressive to *Pythium* and *Rhizoctonia*. As more scientific work is reported, it becomes more evident that there may be general disease suppression with many horticultural and other crops.

In the U.S. nursery industry, control of diseases such as *Phytophthora* root rots with compost has been at least as effective as that obtained with fungicides. In fact, much of the international agricultural community relies heavily on compost for control of diseases caused by these soilborne plant pathogens. Suppression of pathogens and/or disease is largely induced during curing. The following bacteria and fungi have been identified as biocontrol agents in composts:

- *Bacillus* spp.,
- *Enterobacter* spp.,
- *Flavobacterium balustinum,*
- *Pseudomonas* spp.,
- *Streptomyces* spp.,
- *Trichoderma* spp., and
- *Gliocladium virens.*

Of increasing interest to researchers and growers is the use of watery compost extracts or compost "teas" that are prepared from finished composts and sprayed directly onto plant surfaces. These biologically active extracts have been shown to suppress both the germination and growth of plant pathogenic organisms. The most significant factors influencing the effectiveness of the watery compost extracts are age and type of compost used. Composts containing horse and dairy manure show significant antifungal potentials up to nine to twelve months of age.

For Increased Pasture Quality

Compost is being used in intensively managed grazing systems. In these systems, fields are divided into small paddocks, and animals are rotated through the paddocks at rates that optimize the growth rate of both plants and animals. During the winter months, while the animals are in barns, the manure is collected and composted. During the grazing season, manure is spread in the paddock soon after it is vacated. The use of compost in pasture systems offers several advantages over raw manure:

- palatability — Compost does not decrease the palatability of a pasture as raw manure does. This is very important to farmers who no longer produce row crops (where raw manure was generally applied).
- plant numbers — In a pasture that includes legumes, compost will help maintain a high legume population, while raw manure will result in a decrease in legume plants. This difference in plant response may be due to the form of nitrogen available, as the more readily available nitrogen in the manure decreases nodulation in legumes.
- convenience — Because compost is a stable product, it can be applied when it suits the farmer's schedule.

As a Mulch in Fruit Production

If compost is to be used as a mulch on orchards or vineyards, an immature compost with large particles will provide better weed control than a screened, mature compost. The immature compost will help starve the weeds for nutrients, while the larger particles will provide a physical barrier. Partially composted bark is particularly suitable for mulching.

Specific advantages of mulching include:
- regulation of soil temperature and humidity,
- reduced soil erosion,
- improved soil biological activity,
- controlled weed germination, and
- improved soil structure.

Mulching with fresh organic residues as well as composts is recommended in nurseries. Compost, when used as a mulch, has been found to be effective in minimizing the spread of brown rot in peach and nectarine orchards. The disease suppression properties of compost appear to be associated with increased worm populations in the soil (the worms feed on diseased fruit that falls to the ground), and with the growth of yeasts on the mulch that discharge spores that surround and protect the fruit.

Application Rates

Compost has been recommended for use in row crops at rates of up to 20 wet tons (40 cubic yards) per acre, depending on nutrient content, with average applications between 5 and 10 wet tons per acre. If compost is used to improve the physical properties of the soil, it may be necessary to make larger applications of compost, with subsequent much lighter applications or applications made only once every two or three years (depending on crop rotation, climate, and farm objectives). There are no set recommendations for using compost to modify soil structural characteristics such as water-holding capacity, water infiltration rate, compaction, bulk density, and tilth. For pastures and hay/legume crops, application rates of up to 7 wet tons (14 cubic yards) per acre have been used, provided the material is stable.

Compost made from coarse ingredients such as bark with some grit or sand content can be used for soil erosion protection. However, compost used for this purpose should be tested for soluble salts so it may be used at heavy rates — up to 100 wet tons per acre. Compost application rates, especially on heavy soils, should not exceed 100 wet tons per acre or approximately 4.6 cubic yards per 1,000 square feet [100 tons/acre x 1 acre/43,560 square feet x 2 cubic yards/ton x 1,000]. Higher rates make the soil difficult to manage. Most compost contains about 50% water, therefore 100 wet tons of compost is equal to 50 dry tons.

In the production of fall-planted, single-crop strawberries, pumpkins or winter squash are generally planted in the same rows immediately following the final strawberry harvest. Based on soil test results, compost has been used at a rate of 50–150 wet tons per acre for the initial application and at one-quarter to one-third the initial application for successive plantings. In the production of blueberries, unscreened compost or composted mulch is generally applied yearly to keep the soil cool and to supply slow-release nutrients. The mulch is generally applied at 50–75 wet tons per acre.

Recommended upper limits for application have been established to avoid the abusive use of compost. The rate at which compost is applied must be balanced among:

- the prime objective for adding the compost,
- the amount of compost available relative to the area covered,
- the effect of compost on soil salinity, and
- the cost of application relative to the perceived benefits.

When used at or near maximum recommended application rates, compost can supply most of a field crop's nutrient needs through the first growing season. The frequency and amount of compost applied will differ depending on crop needs, field history (recent compost or manure applications will reduce the amount of compost needed), and local climate (see sidebar on page 93). The example at right examines using compost to supply the nutrient needs of a corn crop.

Farm compost may be applied using conventional rear-delivery or side-delivery manure spreaders for covering large acreage. A variety of spinner-type spreaders (figure 6-1, page 94 and photo 2-5) can also be used for field applications of compost. When using spinner or perforated-roller-type spreaders, it is important that the moisture content of the compost be between 40% and 45%. Compost that contains more than 45% moisture will tend to clump and "bridge" in the spreader hopper. Compost containing less than 40% moisture will be very dusty.

NUTRIENT RELEASE FROM COMPOST

Most nutrients in compost are bound to or in organic matter. Mineralization, or release, of these nutrients depends on biological activity. Therefore, rates of nutrient release from composts are temperature dependent. At temperatures below freezing, release is negligible. At temperatures above freezing, release increases in proportion to temperature.

In temperate climates, the rate of mineralization parallels seasonal changes in ambient temperatures, with the greatest nutrient release occurring during summer when plant growth rates are also higher. Composts applied to soils in temperature-controlled conditions or tropical environments often have mineralization rates higher than rates observed in outdoor or temperate climatic conditions.

Mineral fertilizers, on the other hand, are highly soluble with little dependence on temperature changes. Thus, crops in cool soils or spring conditions may grow more slowly with composts as nutrient sources than with soluble fertilizers. However, crops grown in warmer soils may grow equally well with composts or soluble nutrients.

EXAMPLE: Using Compost to Supply Crop Nutrient Needs

Farm compost analysis:

Moisture content 50%
Bulk density .... 1,000 pounds/cubic yard
Total nitrogen (N) .... 1.5% *
Phosphorus (P) .... 0.5% *
Potassium (K) .... 1.0% *

*Nutrient analyses reported on a dry-weight basis

If the above compost is to supply a corn crop with 100 pounds of N per acre, assuming a 12% first-year N mineralization rate, approximately 60 wet tons of compost per acre would be required:

> 60 tons/acre x 50% solids x 2,000 lbs/ton x 1.5%N x 12% first-year mineralization = 108 lbs N/acre

Since the compost has a bulk density of approximately 1,000 pounds per cubic yard, or 2 cubic yards per wet ton, this means that 120 cubic yards of compost would have to be applied per acre to supply the needs of the corn crop. Such an application rate would result in applying 300 total pounds of P and 600 total pounds of K per acre. Repeated applications at this rate may result in excessive levels of P and K being built up in the soil.

If emphasis was placed on meeting the P needs of the corn crop, and assuming a 30% first-year mineralization rate for P and approximately 44 pounds P required per acre of corn production, then only 30 wet tons of compost would be needed per acre:

> 30 tons/acre x 50% solids x 2,000 lbs/ton x 0.5% P x 30% first-year mineralization = 45 lbs P/acre

If compost application rates were based on the P needs of the corn, the N needs of the crop could be satisfied by either applying mineral N or plowing down a legume cover crop. Depending on soil test levels and N, P, and K mineralization rates during successive years, reduced compost applications in the years following can be managed to provide sufficient nutrients to produce successive corn crops while not overapplying P or K.

NOTE: In areas with elevated phosphate levels, land application of compost may be regulated based on phosphorus limitations.

FIGURE 6-1. Field application of compost

Compost can also be land applied on level ground using front-end loaders and land levelers or road graders. Often, when rates of 1 inch or more are applied, piles of compost are placed in strategic locations around the field before spreading. Assuming proper particle size and moisture content, and with experience and care, composts can be spread at accurate field application rates. For small areas, compost can be spread using shovels and rakes. New methods of applying compost or mulch, including equipment for blowing compost through 4-inch flexible hose at up to 60 cubic yards per hour over distances well over 300 feet, have added increased applicability for compost.

Because of the porous and bulky nature of compost, it is often helpful to estimate the volume of compost needed to achieve the coverage desired. Table 6-3 (page 96) converts application rates from wet tons per acre to cubic yards per acre based on compost bulk density and can be used to estimate the volume of compost or mulch required for a specific application rate. Table 6-2 below can be used to convert application rates in cubic yards per acre to a depth of application. Both tables assume no compaction.

TABLE 6-2. Cubic yards per acre for various depths of application

Depth of application (inches)	Cubic yards per acre[a]
¼	34
⅜	50
½	68
¾	101
1	135
1½	202
2	270
2½	336
3	405

[a] Assumes no compaction and uniform and complete coverage.

Example: 1-inch application x (1 foot/12 inches) x (43,560 square feet/1 acre) x (1 cubic yard/27 cubic feet) = 135 cubic yards per acre

EXAMPLE: Determining Compost Application Rate

Use tables 6-2 (page 94) and 6-3 (page 96) to determine the application rate in cubic yards per acre and the application depth in inches.

Given: The desired application rate based on nutrient analysis and crop needs is 12 dry tons of compost per acre. The moisture content of the compost is determined to be 40%. The bulk density of compost is field-measured at 900 pounds per cubic yard .

Required:

Part 1. How many cubic yards of compost are needed per acre?

Part 2. How many inches of compost will be spread at this application rate?

Solution:

Part 1. Based on a 40% moisture content and a required application rate of 12 dry tons per acre, 20 wet tons of compost will be required per acre [12 dry tons ÷ (1.0 – 0.4) = 20 wet tons]. Using table 6-3, and entering both columns for 800 and 1,000 pounds per cubic yard (to obtain an average), the application rates corresponding to 20 wet tons per acre are 50 and 40 cubic yards per acre, respectively. Therefore, the average of the two, or 45 cubic yards per acre, is the volume of compost required.

Part 2. Using table 6-2, a volume of 45 cubic yards per acre, assuming no compaction and uniform and complete coverage, is equal to approximately a ⅜-inch depth of application.

For smaller application areas, determine the cubic yards of compost or mulch required to cover a specific area, in square feet, by using the following formula:

__ square feet x __ inches of compost x 0.0031 = __ cubic yards

Example:

2,000-square-foot garden area x 2 inches of compost x 0.0031 = 12.4 cubic yards (which is equal to 270 cubic yards per acre)

TABLE 6-3. Application rate, in cubic yards per acre, based on bulk density

Tons/acre (wet)	Bulk density (lbs/cu yd)[a]							
	600	800	1,000	1,200	1,400	1,600	1,800	2,000
1.0	3.3	2.5	2.0	1.7	1.4	1.3	1.1	1.0
1.5	5.0	3.8	3.0	2.5	2.1	1.9	1.7	1.5
2.0	6.7	5.0	4.0	3.3	2.9	2.5	2.2	2.0
3.0	10.0	7.5	6.0	5.0	4.3	3.8	3.3	3.0
4.0	13.3	10.0	8.0	6.7	5.7	5.0	4.4	4.0
5.0	16.7	12.5	10.0	8.3	7.1	6.3	5.6	5.0
6.0	20.0	15.0	12.0	10.0	8.6	7.5	6.7	6.0
7.0	23.3	17.5	14.0	11.7	10.0	8.8	7.8	7.0
8.0	26.7	20.0	16.0	13.3	11.4	10.0	8.9	8.0
9.0	30.0	22.5	18.0	15.0	12.9	11.3	10.0	9.0
10.0	33.3	25.0	20.0	16.7	14.3	12.5	11.1	10.0
15.0	50.0	37.5	30.0	25.0	21.4	18.8	16.7	15.0
20.0	66.7	50.0	40.0	33.3	28.6	25.0	22.2	20.0
30.0	100.0	75.0	60.0	50.0	42.9	37.5	33.3	30.0
40.0	—	100.0	80.0	66.7	57.1	50.0	44.4	40.0

continued on next page

TABLE 6-3. Application rate, in cubic yards per acre, based on bulk density *(continued)*

| Tons/acre (wet) | Bulk density (lbs/cu yd)[a] | | | | | | | | |
	600	800	1,000	1,200	1,400	1,600	1,800	2,000
50.0	–	–	100.0	83.3	71.4	62.5	55.6	50.0
60.0	–	–	–	100.0	85.7	75.0	66.7	60.0
80.0	–	–	–	–	–	100.0	88.9	80.0
100.0	–	–	–	–	–	–	–	100.0

Adapted from The Composting Council's *Compost: It's a Natural! – A Farmer's Field Guide to Compost Production and Use*, 1996.

Note: Table assumes no compaction.

[a] For field determination of bulk density, see "Bulking Materials," page 31.

APPENDIX A: Case Study– Land Applying Composted Materials and Uncomposted Yard Trimmings on Highly Erodible Land

This study was written by Scott McCoy of the Texas Natural Resources Conservation Commission and James Greenwade, Homer Sanchez, and Mark Freeman of the USDA Natural Resources Conservation Service.

Approximately 14.7% (by weight) of the municipal solid waste stream presently disposed of in landfills is yard trimmings such as grass clippings, leaves, and tree trimmings. Disposal of these materials costs Texans $250 million annually. These materials have the potential to be reused through composting and direct application onto highly erodible lands to provide needed organic material. Use of composted and uncomposted yard trimmings as a soil amendment can reduce the need for chemical fertilizers and pesticides, and therefore reduce nonpoint source (NPS) pollution.

This demonstration provided comprehensive information on the land application of composted and uncomposted yard trimmings on designated highly erodible lands in Texas. The target areas were identified by the USDA-Natural Resources Conservation Service (NRCS) and the Texas Natural Resource Conservation Commission (TNRCC) as sites where the implementation of best management practices (BMPs), education, and field demonstrations will substantially reduce the potential of field runoff. This would reduce the impact of NPS pollution on surface water and groundwater quality. The project produced technical and educational material in the form of a video, field guide, and site demonstrations.

The partners used EPA 319(h) funds administered through the Texas State Soil and Water Conservation Board to establish four agricultural demonstration sites. The four sites were Big Springs, Pampa, Nacogdoches, and Lubbock. The Lubbock site was for demonstration only, in conjunction with the Texas Farmer Stockman Show. Material was applied at the agricultural demonstration sites at predetermined rates ranging from 5 to 40 tons per acre. The EPA 319(h) funds provided for the testing of samples from demonstration sites for pesticide contamination, crop yields, organic matter, and water quality of runoff. The sites were monitored through soil testing for nitrogen, phosphorus, potassium, micronutrients, organic material, and pesticide residuals. In addition, climatic data and runoff information were compiled at each site to evaluate soil loss, nutrient content, and changes in organic material.

Methodology

Plot Locations
Plots were located near the following cities, all of which agreed to participate in field trials: Pampa, Big Springs, and Nacogdoches.

Soils

Major agricultural soils near the cities were selected. In addition, highly erodible soils were selected to determine the benefits of adding compost or wood chips. Three different soil textures were selected: Amarillo fine sandy loam was selected at the Big Springs site, Mansker clay loam was selected at the Pampa site, and Darco loamy fine sand was selected at the Nacogdoches site.

Plot Design

Test plots were one-quarter acre in size. The corners were permanently marked for reference. Landowners and farmers were asked to farm the fields in a normal manner. No special instructions were given as to what crops to plant or how or when to plant, as we wanted to see the differences made by various application rates and materials.

Plots were located within the soil delineation and on the same soil type. Uniform slopes were selected for all plots. The following plots and application rates were initially established at each location: control; wood chips, 5 tons; wood chips, 10 tons; wood chips, 15 tons; compost, 5 tons; compost, 10 tons; and compost, 15 tons. It appeared that the rate for compost needed to be increased; therefore, the second-year application rates were applied at 20-, 30-, and 40-ton rates. All rates were applied on a dry-weight basis.

Soil Samples for Analysis

Soil samples were taken on all plots to determine the levels of nitrogen; phosphorus; potassium; organic carbon; 2,4-D; and Diazinon. Soil samples were taken from each plot at several locations and composited. Sample depths were 0–6 inches and 6–24 inches on all plots. Materials applied to and water used on the plots were also sampled and tested for the chemicals listed above.

Rainfall Simulator

Since the 1940s, rainfall simulators have been used to emulate natural rainfall in experimental plots. A primary advantage of the small-plot rainfall simulator used by the NRCS is to obtain field data that can be used to compare relative differences between treatments or vegetative types. Rainfall simulators can also provide information to validate model estimates and predictions of intertill soil loss, sedimentation, and water quality. In establishing procedures, the USDA-NRCS Technical Note, "Small Plot Rainfall Simulation: Background and Procedures," dated March 1995, was used.

The rainfall simulator used to collect data for this study is a drip needle rainfall simulator. It is equipped with four legs and extends 2 meters in height. The Plexiglass applicator module contains 3,600 needles on 1.27-centimeter centers with a surface area of 0.58 square meter. Rainfall intensity can be controlled through a flow meter, and rainfall applications can range from 0.5 inch per hour to 6 inches per hour. For this project simulations were made at the 4-inches-per-hour rate. An advantage of this simulator is that water droplets are very evenly distributed over the soil surface.

A minimum of two simulations was applied to each treatment site plus the control sites. When necessary, three simulations were done per site. To eliminate variances relating to time and moisture, all sites were prewet. A standard plot size of 2.03 square feet was used for simulation. The simulator was calibrated prior to each run.

Simulations were run for thirty-minute time periods at a rate of [...] inches per hour. The percent runoff and infiltration rates can be calculated from this data. Runoff find sediment were collected at five-minute intervals, and analyses were made from subsamples for each of the three ten-minute intervals. Runoff samples were analyzed by a laboratory to determine total suspended solids, nitrogen, phosphorus, and potassium.

Yields

Wheat

Forage yields were based on clips and weight using the 1 square meter. Grain production estimates were done according to a Farm Service Agency production appraisal worksheet for small grains.

Cotton

Ten random samples were taken from each plot. Thirteen-foot lengths were measured, and the open bolls were counted. The number was multiplied by the average boll weight of 1.36 grams lint. The total was divided by 457 grams (number of grams in a pound). This was multiplied by 1,000, which resulted in pounds of lint per acre. These methods were utilized on the control, compost, and wood chip plots.

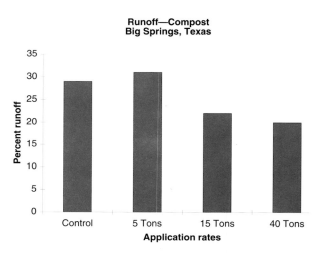

CHART 1. Runoff rates for this Amarillo fine sandy loam soil at Big Springs, Texas show a positive effect from applications of compost material. Applications with as much as 40 tons of compost per acre showed that infiltration increased and runoff decreased. The Pampa, Texas site (chart 2), where the soil was a considerably tighter Mansker clay loam, showed that applications of compost at rates greater than 5 tons per acre actually increased the amount of runoff for each trial. Higher rates of fine compost material may have caused a quicker sealing of the soil surface. This result can be lessened by incorporating the compost material. However, by the second year, the sites with applications of compost greater than 10 tons per acre showed runoff rates beginning to decrease due to compost material decomposition.

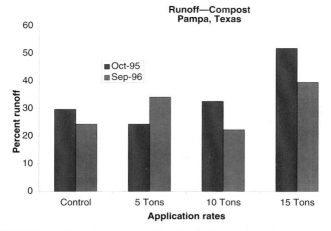

CHART 2. Runoff rates for compost on Mansker clay loam soil were lowest for the 5-ton rate but increased with heavier applications as the surface sealed. Note that the second year the lowest runoff was on the 10-ton plot as the compost began to decompose and was incorporated through tillage.

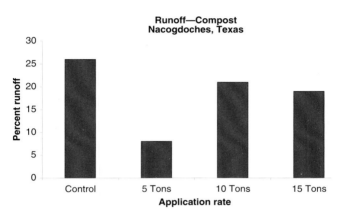

CHART 3. Compost application on Darco loamy fine sand. Runoff was reduced about 65% at the 5-ton rate, about 20% at the 10-ton rate, and about 25% at the 15-ton rate. The maximum benefit for the year of application was at the 5-ton rate; however, as the compost decomposes, the higher rates of application will provide longer lasting benefit.

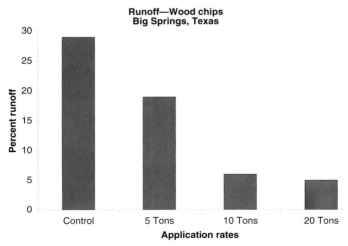

CHART 4. The addition of wood chips on this Amarillo fine sandy loam soil showed a reduction in runoff at all rates. The highest reduction was with rates of 20 tons per acre. A greater than 80% reduction in runoff occurred between the 20-ton rate and the control field.

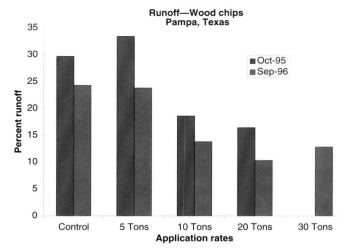

CHART 5. Wood chip application on Mansker clay loam. Very little change occurred between the control and the 5-ton rate. The highest reduction was at the 10- and 20-ton rates. It appears from this data that the maximum benefit is at 20 tons. However, in future years, even the 30-ton rate will show positive benefits. Notice also that a further reduction in runoff rates occurs between the first and second year on the same treatments due to wood chip decomposition.

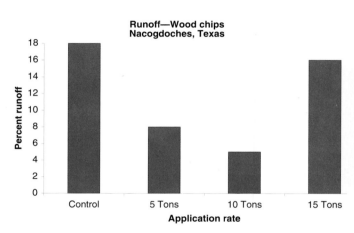

CHART 6. Wood chip application on Darco loamy fine sand. Runoff was reduced about 55% at the 5-ton rate and about 70% at the 10-ton rate. Wood chips at the 15-ton rate showed a slight reduction in the year of application, but long-term benefits will likely be greater.

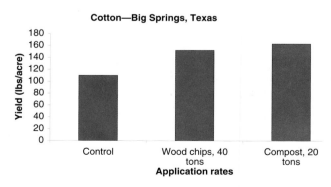

CHART 7. Yield data for cotton crop harvested during fall of 1997 on Amarillo fine sandy loam soil. Data show that both the wood chips and the compost trials increased yields over the control plot. The highest yield was on the 20-ton-per-acre compost plot.

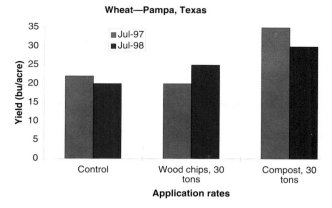

CHART 8. Wheat on Mansker clay loam harvested in July 1997. The highest yield was on those plots with 30 tons of compost. Approximately a 50% increase in yield was obtained over the control plot with compost at 20 tons per acre. A slight decrease in yield was obtained when using high rates of wood chips during the first year after application. It is felt that as the wood chips break down, the yield could possibly increase.

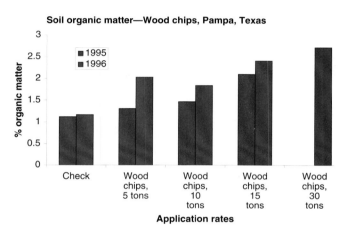

CHART 9. Soil organic matter increased with higher application rates of wood chips at the Pampa site. As the wood chips decompose to stable organic matter, the soil organic matter increased slightly from 1995 to 1996 with no additional materials being applied. Similar results were obtained at the Big Springs and Nacogdoches sites.

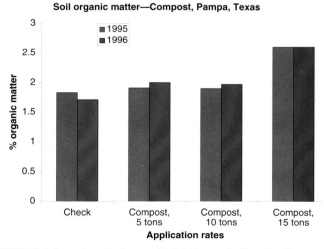

CHART 10. Soil organic matter increased with higher application rates of compost on the plots at Pampa. Organic matter increased from 1995 to 1996 as the compost decomposed to stable organic matter. Similar results were obtained at Big Springs and Nacogdoches.

Summary

Soil erosion robs the landscape of more than three billion tons of topsoil each year. A large amount of this erosion takes place on lands that are highly erodible. Runoff from depleted soils can increase siltation and contribute to agricultural nonpoint source pollution. Pesticides, fertilizers, and field residues are carried into our nation's water supply due to water erosion.

Another problem that is affecting urban and rural citizens is inadequate space for landfills. Therefore, it is imperative that we recycle and extend the useful life of our existing landfills.

This project demonstrated a win-win situation for the urban, rural, and agricultural communities. Applying composted yard trimmings and uncomposted wood chips to highly erodible land in Texas provided beneficial results in addressing the problems stated above. Highlights of the study included:

1. Composted materials were tested for pathogens and chemical and fertilizer residuals. All tests indicated that none were present.

2. Yields increased on all plots compared to the check plots. Compost acts as a water reservoir in the soil, increasing water-holding capacity.

3. Organic matter increased slightly the first year of the demonstration. Greater results were obtained the second and third years due to decomposition of the material.

4. Infiltration rates increased and runoff decreased. Compost used as a soil amendment reduces soil erosion and runoff by acting as the glue that holds the soil particles together.

Best management practices identified during the demonstration showed that a 30- to 40-ton rate of composted material and a 15- to 20-ton rate of wood chips that are chipped to about the size of a quarter are optimal. Results were greater when material was disked or tucked into the top layer of the soil profile, as compared to being surface applied.

Farmers benefit from application of this material because of higher yields, less chemical use, erosion control, and increased organic matter. Developing the agricultural and urban markets, developing equipment for large-scale application, and determining the economic feasibility of hauling the material over extended distances are issues that still need to be addressed.

This project demonstrated that land application is a feasible alternative to dumping yard trimmings such as grass, leaves, and tree trimmings into our landfills. Cities that compost yard trimmings have limited markets. Agricultural land provides a large-scale market for this material.

For more information about this project, contact:

Scott McCoy
Texas Natural Resource Conservation Commission
P.O. Box 13087
Austin, Texas 78711
(512) 239-6774

APPENDIX B: Metric Conversions

TABLE B-1. Metric conversions

| Type of unit | From U.S. Customary System Units | | To SI (metric) units | | Multiply by |
	Unit	Abbreviation	Unit	Abbreviation	U.S. to SI conversion factor
Area	acre	acre	hectare	ha	0.4047
	square foot	ft²	square meter	m²	0.0929
	square inch	in²	square centimeter	cm²	6.4516
	square mile	mile²	square kilometer	km²	2.5900
Conductance, electric	mho	mho	siemens	S	1
Density (mass)	pounds per cubic foot	lb/ft³	kilograms per cubic meter	kg/m³	16.0185
	pounds per cubic inch	lb/in³	kilograms per cubic meter	kg/m³	27,679.90
	pounds per cubic yard	lb/yd³	kilograms per cubic meter	kg/m³	0.5933
Energy	British thermal unit	Btu	kilojoule	kJ	1.0551
	foot-pound	ft-lbf	joule	J	1.3558
	kilocalorie	kcal	kilojoule	kJ	4.1868
Flow volume	cubic feet per second	ft³/s	cubic meters per minute	m³/min	1.6990
	cubic feet per second	ft³/s	cubic meters per second	m³/s	0.0283
	gallons per hour	gal/h or gph	liters per hour	L/h	3.7854
	gallons per minute	gal/min or gpm	liters per minute	L/min	3.7854
	gallons per second	gal/s or gps	cubic meters per second	m³/s	0.0037854
	gallons per second	gal/s or gps	liters per second	L/s	3.7854

continued on next page

TABLE B-1. Metric conversions *(continued)*

Type of unit	From U.S. Customary System Units			To SI (metric) units			Multiply by
	Unit	Abbreviation		Unit	Abbreviation		U.S. to SI conversion factor
Length	foot	ft		meter	m		0.3048
	inch	in		centimeter	cm		2.54
	micron	micron		micrometer	μm		1
	mile	mile		kilometer	km		1.6093
	yard	yd		meter	m		0.9144
Mass	ounce	oz		gram	g		28.3495
	pound	lb		kilogram	kg		0.4536
	ton (long)	ton		ton, Megagram	t, Mg		1.016
	ton (short)	ton		ton, Megagram	t, Mg		0.9072

Note: The symbol t is used to designate metric ton. The unit metric ton (exactly 1 Mg, or 1 million grams) is in wide use, but its applications are limited.

Mass per time	ton (short) per hour	ton/h		t or Megagram per hour	t/h, Mg/h		0.9072
Power	horsepower	hp		kilowatt	kW		0.7457
Pressure	inches of water	in H$_2$O		kilopascals	kPa		0.2488
Temperature	degrees Fahrenheit	°F		degrees Celsius (Centigrade)	°C		$t_C = (t_F - 32) \div 1.8$

continued on next page

TABLE B-1. Metric conversions *(continued)*

Type of unit	From U.S. Customary System Units		To SI (metric) units		Multiply by
	Unit	Abbreviation	Unit	Abbreviation	U.S. to SI conversion factor
Velocity	feet per minute	ft/min or fpm	meters per minute	m/min	0.3048
	feet per second	ft/s	meters per second	m/s	0.3048
	inches per second	in/s	millimeters per second	mm/s	25.4
	miles per hour	mile/hour or mph	kilometers per hour	km/h	1.6093
Volume	bushel	bushel	liter	L	35.2391
	cubic foot	ft³	cubic meter	m³	0.0283
	cubic yard	yd³	cubic meter	m³	0.7646
	gallon	gal	liter	L	3.7854
	ounce	oz	milliliter	mL	29.5735
	pint	pt	liter	L	0.4732
	quart	qt	liter	L	0.9464

PHOTOGRAPHS

PHOTO 1a Loader lifting and turning *(Bruce Fulford)*

PHOTO 1b Various pieces of equipment *(Jack Pos)*

PHOTO 1c Small one-pass windrow turner (California) *(Robert Rynk)*

PHOTO 1d Windrow turner *(Robert Rynk)*

PHOTO 1e Aerated static piles *(Sukhu Mathur)*

PHOTO 1f "Ag-bag" composting system *(compliments of Ag-bag)*

PHOTO 1g Rotating drum vessel on a dairy (Texas) *(Don Cawthon)*

PHOTO 1-1 Windrows on a dairy (Texas) *(Robert Rynk)*

PHOTO 1-2 Straight windrows on a farm *(Robert Rynk)*

PHOTO 1-3 Dump truck moving heated material *(Robert Rynk)*

PHOTO 1-4 Homemade trommel screen (Canada) *(Robert Rynk)*

PHOTO 1-5 Compost storage shed *(Robert Rynk)*

PHOTO 2-1 Pile of straw (Idaho) *(Robert Rynk)*

PHOTO 2-2 Tare dirt and onion culls *(Robert Rynk)*

PHOTO 2-3 Potato culls *(John MacLeod and Roger Henry)*

PHOTO 2-4 Cranberry processing waste *(Maarten van de Kamp)*

PHOTO 2-5 Spreader with spinners *(Robert Rynk)*

PHOTO 2-6 Shovelful of compost *(Robert Rynk)*

PHOTO 3-1 Moisture addition while turning at a dairy (Texas) *(Robert Rynk)*

PHOTO 3-2 Active composting site in winter *(Robert Rynk)*

PHOTO 3-3 Maturity tests *(Robert Rynk)*

PHOTO 3-4 Wet site conditions (advantage of a paved site) *(Robert Rynk)*

PHOTO 4-1 Runoff collection ditch *(Robert Rynk)*

PHOTO 5-1 Bin composting (Maryland) *(Robert Rynk)*

REFERENCES

Alexander, Ronald A. "Standards and Guidelines for Compost Use." In *Farm Scale Composting*. Emmaus, Pennsylvania: JG Press, Inc. 1995.

Arble, William C. and Dennis J. Murphy. *Extinguishing Silo Fires* (NRAES–18). Ithaca, New York: Northeast Regional Agricultural Engineering Service. 1989.

ASAE. *Standards, Engineering Practices, and Data.* 38th Edition. St. Joseph, Michigan: American Society of Agricultural Engineers. 1991.

Baker, L. Dale, William E. Field, Rollin Schnieder, Clair W. Young, Robert A. Parsons, and Dennis J. Murphy. *Farm Accident Rescue* (NRAES–10). Ithaca, New York: Northeast Regional Agricultural Engineering Service. 1986.

Beierlein, J., Jayson Harper, and Cary Oshins. *Marketing On-Farm Compost.* Extension Circular 423. State College, Pennsylvania: The Pennsylvania State University, College of Agricultural Sciences. 1996.

BioCycle staff (Ed.). "Odor Control at Composting Sites." In *Composting Source Separated Organics*. Emmaus, Pennsylvania: JG Press, Inc. 1994.

BioCycle staff. "Financing Options for Composting Firms." *BioCycle* (November 1996).

Brinton, William F. (Ed.). *Earth, Plant, and Compost: Principles of Composting for Garden and Farm*. Mount Vernon, Maine: Woods End Agricultural Institute, Inc. 1995.

Brinton, William F. Class notes. University of Maine Cooperative Extension Compost School. Orono, Maine: University of Maine Cooperative Extension. August 25–29, 1997.

Brodie, Herbert L. and Lewis E. Carr. "Composting Animal Mortalities on Farms." In *Farm Scale Composting*. Emmaus, Pennsylvania: JG Press, Inc. 1995.

Brodie, Herbert L. and Lewis E. Carr. "Composting Animal Mortality." Paper presented at ORBIT 97 Conference, Harrogate, United Kingdom, September 2–3, 1997.

Brodie, Herbert L., Francis R. Gouin, and Lewis E. Carr. "What Makes Good Compost?" In *Farm Scale Composting*. Emmaus, Pennsylvania: JG Press, Inc. 1995.

Composting Council. *Compost: It's a Natural! A Farmer's Field Guide to Compost Production and Use*. Slide chart. Alexandria, Virginia: The Composting Council. 1996.

Composting Council. *Field Guide to Compost Use*. Alexandria, Virginia: The Composting Council. 1996.

Composting Council. *Potential U.S. Applications for Compost*. Alexandria, Virginia: The Composting Council. 1992.

Composting Council. *Suggested Compost Parameters and Compost Use Guidelines*. Composting Council Fact Sheet. Alexandria, Virginia: The Composting Council. 1995.

Conner, D. E., J. P. Blake, and J. O. Donald. "Microbiological Safety of Composted Poultry Farm Mortalities." Paper 91-4053. St. Joseph, Michigan: American Society of Agricultural Engineers. 1991.

Cornell University. Cornell Composting Web Page. URL (current as of 3-21-98): HTTP://WWW.CFE.CORNELL.EDU/COMPOST/DOWNLOAD.HTML. [Downloadable spreadsheets available for simultaneous solution of compost recipes using up to four ingredients. Spreadsheets are available in either Macintosh or DOS/Windows format using Excel or Lotus.]

Cotton, Matthew. "Composting Moves West." *Waste Age* (May 1996).

Crockett, John. "The Importance of Oxygen." *BioCycle* (May 1997).

Diener, Robert G. Class notes. Commercial Composting (Agricultural and Environmental Education 280-A). Morgantown, West Virginia: West Virginia University. Spring 1998.

Dougherty, Mark (Ed.). *Composting for Municipalities: Planning and Design Considerations* (NRAES–94). Ithaca, New York: Natural Resource, Agriculture, and Engineering Service. 1998.

Epstein, Eliot. (Ed.) "Composting and Bioaerosols." In *Composting Source Separated Organics*. Emmaus, Pennsylvania: JG Press, Inc. 1994.

Franklin Associates, Ltd. *Characterization of Municipal Solid Waste in the United States, 1996 Update*. Prepared for the U.S. Environmental Protection Agency. Prairie Village, Kansas. 1997.

Fulhage, C. and C. Ells. "Composting Dead Swine." Fact Sheet WQ225. University of Missouri Cooperative Extension Service. Columbia, Missouri: University of Missouri. 1994.

Glenn, Jim. "Living Up to the Good Neighbor Policy." *BioCycle* (August 1997).

Glenn, Jim. "300,000,000 Tons of Manure." *BioCycle* (January 1998).

Glenn, Jim and Molly Farrell. "Bagging and Blending Strengthen Compost Markets." *BioCycle* (July 1997).

Goldstein, Jerome. "Safety at Composting Facilities." *BioCycle* (March 1997).

Goldstein, Nora. "Checking Out the Pad." *BioCycle* (October 1996).

Gouin, Francis R. Class notes. 5th Annual Better Composting School. Hanover, Maryland: University of Maryland Foundation, Inc. October 29–November 1, 1996.

Graves, W. E. "On-Farm Methods for Composting Livestock Carcasses." University of Massachusetts Extension Agroecology, vol. 2, no. 1 (Spring 1997).

Graves, William E. "Composting Systems." Electronic posting to DAIRY-L dairy discussion list (DAIRY_L@UMDD.UMD.EDU). October 1997.

Greaser, G. and J. Harper. *Enterprise Budget Analysis*. Agricultural Alternatives Series. State College, Pennsylvania: Penn State Cooperative Extension. 1994.

Grobe, Karen. "It's a New Era for Farm Compost." *BioCycle* (May 1997).

Haug, Roger T. "Feedstocks, Conditioning, and Fire Protection." *BioCycle* (April 1997).

Haynes, John. "Applying Compost and Mulches to Control Erosion." *BioCycle* (May 1997).

Hillers, Val. "Manures and Pathogens to Humans." Electronic posting to DAIRY-L dairy discussion list (DAIRY_L@UMDD.UMD.EDU). November 1997.

Hoitink, H. A. J., H. M. Keener, and C. R. Krause. "Management Principles." In *Composting Source Separated Organics*. Emmaus, Pennsylvania: JG Press, Inc. 1994.

Hoitink, Harry A. and Marcella E. Grebus. "Status of Biological Control of Plant Diseases with Composts." *Compost Science and Utilization* (Spring 1994).

Kashmanian, Richard M. "The Right Time for Composting in Agriculture." In *Farm Scale Composting.* Emmaus, Pennsylvania: JG Press, Inc. 1995.

Kashmanian, Richard M. and Robert F. Rynk. "Creating Positive Incentives for Farm Composting." *American Journal of Alternative Agriculture,* vol. 13, no. 1 (1998).

Kashmanian, Richard M. and Robert F. Rynk. "Agricultural Composting in the United States: Trends and Driving Forces." *Journal of Soil and Water Conservation* (May–June 1996).

Majercak, John, Daren Bouquillon, and Sherill Baldwin. "Expanding On-Farm Composting." *BioCycle* (January 1998).

Maynard, Abigail A. "Sustained Vegetable Production for Three Years Using Composted Animal Manures." *Compost Science and Utilization,* vol. 2, no. 1 (1994).

Morris J., T. O'Conner, and F. Kains. "A Method for the Bio-Degradation of Dead Pigs." In *Proceedings of the Seventh International Symposium on Agricultural and Food Processing Wastes.* St. Joseph, Michigan: American Society of Agricultural Engineers. 1995.

Murphy, D. W. "Disease Transfer Studies in a Dead Bird Composter." In *Proceedings of the 1990 National Poultry Waste Management Symposium.* Auburn University, Auburn, Alabama: National Poultry Waste Symposium Committee. 1990.

Murphy, D. W. "Minicomposter Dead Bird Disposal." Fact Sheet 642. College Park, Maryland: University of Maryland Cooperative Extension Service. 1992.

Murphy, D. W. "New Developments in Mortality Composters." In *Proceedings of the 1992 National Poultry Waste Management Symposium.* Auburn University, Auburn, Alabama: National Poultry Waste Symposium Committee. 1992.

Murphy, Dennis W. and Lewis E. Carr. "Composting Dead Birds." Fact Sheet 537. College Park, Maryland: University of Maryland Cooperative Extension Service. 1991.

Murphy, D. W. and T. S. Handwerker. "Preliminary Investigations of Composting as a Method of Dead Bird Disposal." In *Proceedings of the 1988 National Poultry Waste Management Symposium.* Ohio State University, Columbus, Ohio: National Poultry Waste Management Symposium Committee. 1988.

Murphy, D. W., M. J. Estienne, C. N. Dobbins, and K. A. Foster. "Disposing of Dead Swine." PIH-133. West Lafayette, Indiana: Purdue University Cooperative Extension Service. 1995.

Northeast Regional Agricultural Engineering Service. *On-Farm Large-Scale Chicken Carcass Composting* (NRAES–110). Video. Ithaca, New York: Northeast Regional Agricultural Engineering Service. 1992.

Pitt, Ron E. *Silage and Hay Preparation* (NRAES–5). Ithaca, New York: Northeast Regional Agricultural Engineering Service. 1990.

Richard, Tom L. "Municipal Solid Waste Composting: Physical and Biological Processing." *Biomass and Bioenergy,* vol. 3, nos. 3-4 (1992): 163–180.

Richard, Tom L. "Water Quality Protection." URL (current as of 7-3-97): HTTP://WWW.CFE.CORNELL.EDU/COMPOST/WATERQUAL.HTML.

Riggle, David. "Why Farmers Become Composters." In *Farm Scale Composting.* Emmaus, Pennsylvania: JG Press, Inc. 1995.

Riggle, David. "Controlling and Preventing Fires at Compost Facilities." *BioCycle* (May 1996).

Riggle, David. "Hard Surface Alternatives." *BioCycle* (November 1997).

Ringer, C. E., P. D. Millner, L. M. Teerlinck, and B. W. Lyman. "Suppression of Seedling Damping-off Disease in Potting Mix Containing Animal Manure Composts." *Compost Science and Utilization,* vol. 5, no. 2 (1997).

Rosenburg, Darlene. "Composting Equipment." *MSW Management.* Santa Barbara, California: Forester Communications, Inc. May/June 1997.

Rynk, Robert (Ed.). *On-Farm Composting Handbook* (NRAES–54). Ithaca, New York: Northeast Regional Agricultural Engineering Service. 1992.

Rynk, Robert. "Dairy Farmers Shift to Composting." In *Farm Scale Composting.* Emmaus, Pennsylvania: JG Press, Inc. 1995.

Rynk, Robert and Michael Colt. *Composting at Home.* CIS-1066. Moscow, Idaho: Ag Communications, The University of Idaho College of Agriculture. 1997.

Seekins, Bill. Class notes. University of Maine Cooperative Extension Compost School. Orono, Maine: University of Maine Cooperative Extension. August 25–29, 1997.

Sikora, L. J. and M. I. Azad. "Effect of Compost-Fertilizer Combinations on Wheat Yields." *Compost Science and Utilization,* vol. 1, no. 2 (1993).

Sussman, V. *Easy Composting.* Emmaus, Pennsylvania: Rodale Press. 1984.

Tchobanoglous, G., H. Theisen, and S. Vigil. *Integrated Solid Waste Management — Engineering Principles and Management Issues.* New York, New York: McGraw-Hill, Inc. 1993.

Turner, Larry W. "Geotextile Feeding/Traffic Surfaces and Costs." AEU-85. Lexington, Kentucky: University of Kentucky Cooperative Extension Service.

Tyler, Rodney W. *Winning the Organics Game: The Compost Marketer's Handbook.* Alexandria, Virginia: The American Society of Horticultural Science (ASHS) Press. 1996.

University of Maryland Cooperative Extension. *Compost Recipe Maker.* Herb Brodie. [Computer spreadsheet program with the capacity to input up to ten selected ingredients, includes database of feedstocks and characteristics. *Compost Recipe Maker (CRM)* is available for a fee in PC-DOS format only. Contact: Biological Resources Engineering Department, University of Maryland, College Park, Maryland 20742-5711.]

van de Kamp, Maarten. Personal communication. October 1997.

Vogtmann, H., K. Matthies, B. Kehres, and A. Meier-Ploeger. "Enhanced Food Quality: Effects of Composts on the Quality of Plant Foods." *Compost Science and Utilization* (Premier Issue, 1993).

Wilmink, Tom. "Managing Odors Associated with Composting." Barboursville, West Virginia: Wilmink Associates, Inc. 1998.